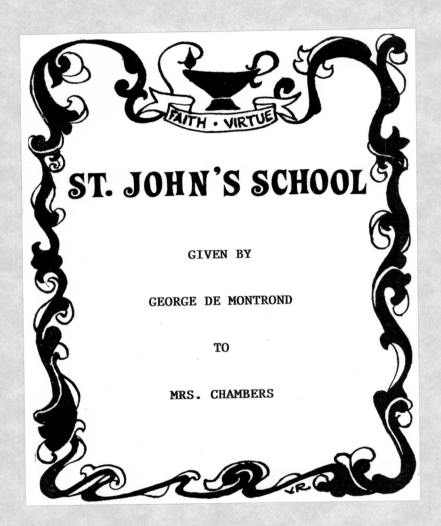

FAITH · VIRTUE

# ST. JOHN'S SCHOOL

GIVEN BY

GEORGE DE MONTROND

TO

MRS. CHAMBERS

# THE MARCH ON WASHINGTON

**Also by James Haskins:**

Black Theater in America

Black Music in America:
*A History Through Its People*

Black Dance in America:
*A History Through Its People*

# JAMES HASKINS

# THE MARCH ON WASHINGTON

**Illustrated with photographs**

**Introduction by
James Farmer**

HarperCollins*Publishers*

Library of Congress Cataloging-in-Publication Data
Haskins, James, date
    The march on Washington : illustrated with photographs / James Haskins ;
introduction by James Farmer.
        p.      cm.
    Includes bibliographical references and index.
    Summary: Discusses the people and events connected with the 1963 March
on Washington, as well as the consequences of this well-known civil rights
demonstration.
    ISBN 0-06-021289-6. — ISBN 0-06-021290-X (lib. bdg.)
    1. March on Washington for Jobs and Freedom, Washington, D.C., 1963—
Juvenile literature.   2. Civil rights demonstrations—Washington (D.C.)—
History—20th century—juvenile literature.   3. Afro-Americans—Civil rights—
Juvenile literature.   [1. March on Washington for Jobs and Freedom,
Washington, D.C., 1963.   2. Civil rights demonstrations.
3. Afro-Americans—Civil rights.]   I. Title.
F200.H35   1993                                              92-13626
323.1'196073'09046—dc20                                          CIP
                                                                 AC

## Acknowledgments

I am grateful to Walter Naegle and
the Bayard Rustin Fund, to Patricia Allen,
and to Kathy Benson for their help.

*To Pat and Fred*

# CONTENTS

# INTRODUCTION

The March on Washington was an idea whose time had come at last. It was first conceived by A. Philip Randolph twenty-two years earlier, in 1941, as a March on Washington for Jobs and Freedom. He called it off when President Franklin D. Roosevelt agreed to issue Executive Order 8802 setting up the first Fair Employment Practices Commission. When Randolph revived the idea of a march on Washington in the early 1960s, many of us wanted to support him.

As you will read later in this book, a lot of negotiating went on before the various civil rights organizations would agree to cooperate on such a march. Many rivalries and differences in style among the leaders of these organizations had to be overcome. At the time I was national director of the Congress of Racial Equality (CORE) and I had every intention of participating in the March on Washington on August 28, 1963. But during the summer of 1963 CORE was engaged in a campaign against segregation in Louisiana, and just a few days before the March on Washington I led a protest march in the town of Plaquemine, in the parish of Iberville, Louisiana. About 230 people participated, and we were all arrested there together.

That put me in a quandary: How was I going to attend the March on Washington? I could have been bailed out, but that would have meant leaving the others in jail. Many of them wanted to go to the March, but CORE did not have enough money to bail everyone out. I felt it would not be proper to bail out alone. Roy Wilkins (head of the National Association for the Advancement of Colored People) and Whitney Young (head of the National Urban League) sent me a wire urging me to come. But I remained in jail—I made the choice to stay with the other protesters. I do not regret that choice.

However, I think it was the worst political decision I ever made. I should have been on that stage at the March on Washington. I sent a message that was read to the marchers by Floyd McKissick, national chairman of CORE, and that you will be able to read in this book. But having a message read for me was not the same as being there. That was a once-in-a-lifetime opportunity to speak live to a worldwide audience. It had never come before and it would never come again.

While the impact of the March on Washington was tremendous, it turned out to be the end of the nonviolent civil rights movement. It was in one sense the last great action of the middle class, for the poor people were not there. The marchers were middle class people: well-paid labor union workers who had cars, middle class whites and blacks. But the poor blacks were not there. They listened to the march on the radio or watched it on television and they were skeptical. They did not go for interracialism and they did not believe in nonviolence. They believed in Malcolm X, who said blacks should claim equal rights "by any means necessary."

The March on Washington attracted more young people to the movement. I, and CORE, responded by recruiting from the streets. So did SNCC (Student Nonviolent Coordinating Committee). But when these young people began moving into CORE and SNCC chapters, a more militant philosophy took hold. That's when people started to move in other directions and the black power movement began. Those who had been committed to nonviolence stepped back. They said, "Look, we pulled off the March on Washington." For them, the fire was gone. It was the end of the nonviolent movement.

But the March on Washington was a signal event in the African-American struggle—the largest peaceful demonstration for racial equality in American history and both an end and a beginning. It is hard for young people to understand what it was like to live in those times. This book puts you there.

—JAMES FARMER
former national director of CORE,
distinguished visiting professor of
history and American studies,
Mary Washington College, Virginia

# THE MARCH ON WASHINGTON

# CHAPTER 1

# THERE WAS A TIME . . .

There was a time in the American South when there were laws preventing black children from going to school with white children. They had to go to separate schools, which were often small and unheated. They had to use books and sports equipment that were castoffs from the white schools. There were no school buses for black children, only for white children.

Black children could not use public libraries, pools, or parks. Black adults could not get good jobs. Black adults were not allowed to vote. They had no voice in the election of the officials who passed the laws that governed their lives.

Many of the laws that governed life in the South were laws of segregation—separating the races. Throughout Southern cities there were signs that read White and Colored. These signs designated separate facilities for each race: public drinking fountains and restrooms, bus station entrances and the buses themselves, movie theaters and sports arenas.

The races were separated in other ways by custom. Black people were expected to call white people Mr. and Mrs. and Miss, while white people called black people by their first names. Blacks were supposed to step aside when whites passed by. A black person could be arrested for talking back to, or "sassing," a white person.

This time in the American South was not the time of slavery. It was one hundred years after slavery had ended. But blacks were still not free.

Life for blacks in the North was better than in the South, but Northern blacks lived under difficult conditions too. They did not have to live under the Southern system of legal segregation. But they suffered from discrimination that kept them from getting good jobs and having equal opportunities with whites.

Since the end of slavery, black people in both the North and the South had often tried to win their civil rights, or full rights of citizenship, and real freedom. In 1892 Homer Plessy brought suit against the Louisiana railroad company that forced him to sit in a segregated car. His case went all the way to the United States Supreme Court, which ruled in 1896 in *Plessy v. Ferguson* that segregation was constitutional as long as "separate but equal" facilities were provided to blacks and whites.

In 1917 ten thousand blacks marched down Fifth Avenue in New York City to protest racial discrimination. In the 1920s Chicago blacks staged a "Jobs-For-Negroes" campaign. In 1936 the National Association for the Advancement of Colored People (NAACP) began to bring suit in Southern courts for equal pay for black teachers.

In the 1940s the Congress of Racial Equality (CORE) staged sit-in demonstrations for integration at a Chicago restaurant and tested segregation policies on interstate bus lines. Blacks in New York demonstrated for and won the right to be hired at white-owned Harlem businesses and local utility companies. Mass meetings were held to protest discrimination in the national defense effort during World War II.

Blacks had sometimes won small gains, but they still did not enjoy the basic rights of citizenship that white people took for granted. In a democracy like the United States, the majority rules, and whites are in the majority. Blacks even today are only eleven percent of the population. In order for blacks to gain their civil rights, they had to make most whites believe they were entitled to them.

That is what the civil rights movement of the 1950s and '60s hoped to accomplish. By demanding their rights through peaceful protest, but not resorting to violence when whites tried to break up their demonstrations, blacks challenged the conscience of white America. They forced whites to see them as human beings just like themselves and to see that their cause was right.

The March on Washington was a high point in the civil rights movement. It was the largest demonstration for human rights in the history of the United States. It was also the largest demonstration that had ever occurred in the nation's capital. Other events had drawn more spectators than the estimated 250,000 people who attended that historic event on Wednesday, August 28, 1963, but no other event had attracted as many actual participants.

The march was also the largest peaceful demonstration in Washington, D.C., to date. In the day-long event just three arrests were made. Not only was it a peaceful march, it was an integrated march. Of the quarter of a million marchers, as many as 60,000 were white.

But it was primarily a black march, and it had been the idea of a black man. That made it another first. The March on Washington was the largest organized Negro political event that had ever been supported by the white power structure. In this case, the power structure was the President and Congress of the United States.

A civil rights bill guaranteeing the basic rights of citizenship to blacks had been introduced by President John F. Kennedy. One goal of the march was to pressure Congress to pass it.

But in a larger sense, the power structure included all white Americans who had sat silently by while ten percent of the population were treated like second-class citizens—if indeed they could be called citizens at all in more than name—just because of the color of their skin.

This is the story of the March on Washington, how it came to be, and how it made history.

**Asa Philip Randolph**

# CHAPTER 2

# A. PHILIP RANDOLPH AND THE CIVIL RIGHTS MOVEMENT

The March on Washington was the idea of A. Philip Randolph, who was seventy-four years old in 1963. He had been working most of his life to win human rights for black people. He had participated in many marches. He had even planned a huge march on the Capitol twenty-two years before. But not until 1963 did his dream come true.

Asa Philip Randolph was born on April 15, 1889, in Crescent City, Florida. His father was a pastor in the local African Methodist Episcopal (A.M.E.) Church. The Randolphs were poor, as were most Southern blacks in the late nineteenth century. Moreover, because they were black, they suffered severe discrimination.

After the Civil War, Union (Northern) troops had occupied the former Confederate (Southern) states until they could write new constitutions. During that time, which was called Reconstruction, Union troops tried to help former slaves get the education and some of the rights that had been denied to them. Many blacks were able to vote, and some blacks were even elected to local and state offices and to the U.S. Congress.

But after the Union troops pulled out, the Southern states quickly took steps to reduce the status of former slaves back to near-slavery. White segregationists terrorized blacks, making them too afraid to exercise their rights. It was at this time that the dreaded Ku Klux Klan arose, frightening blacks with their white-hooded robes and cross burnings. Lynchings, or mob killings, of blacks increased. Laws were passed that segregated blacks from whites in every area of life. These laws were called Jim Crow laws, after a minstrel character of the time—a white man who performed in blackface and who called himself Jim Crow.

As a boy, Randolph heard stories of white violence and lynchings. But he was fortunate enough also to know that it was possible for blacks to stand up to whites and to their violent threats. He was nine years old when a white mob threatened to seize a black man from the local county jail and lynch him. A group of black men decided to prevent that from happening. Randolph later recalled that the men "stood all night like sentries in the street and kept the lynch mob from coming. I'll never forget it. It had a tremendous effect on me."

Another powerful influence on the young Randolph came a few years later when he read *The Souls of Black Folk* by W.E.B. Du Bois. William Edward Burghardt Du Bois had been the first black student to receive a Ph.D. from Harvard University. He later helped to found the National Association for the Advancement of Colored People

and was the editor of its newspaper, *Crisis*. He wrote many books and articles about blacks. From *The Souls of Black Folk* Randolph learned that his people had not only courage and strength but also talent and intelligence, and that the most talented and intelligent people had a responsibility to lead others.

Like many blacks, A. Philip Randolph fled the South and headed north looking for a better life. In 1911, at the age of twenty-two, he went to New York and settled in Harlem. He attended City College, paying his way with money earned from various unskilled jobs. There was not the severe segregation in the North that existed in the South, but blacks still faced discrimination. Only unskilled jobs were open to them, and the black workers were often treated badly. Randolph frequently protested and was usually fired for stirring up trouble.

Meanwhile, at City College, he was learning about socialism. Socialism is a political system designed to foster the economic equality of citizens through government ownership and control of industry and its products. First developed in 1839 in Europe, the idea of socialism was a reaction to the economic and social changes that accompanied the Industrial Revolution. When machines began to replace workers, factory owners quickly grew rich, while factory workers became increasingly poor. Such an economic system, in which ownership of production is in private hands, is called capitalism. It is the system we use in the United States.

Socialism advocated taking factory ownership out of the hands of individuals and placing it in government hands, to assure a more even sharing of the wealth of the nation. Randolph believed that socialism was the only way black workers could enjoy economic equality, and he vowed to spend his life helping black workers.

In 1914 Randolph married Lucille Green. She was an unusual black woman for two reasons: She had a thriving beauty-shop business, and she was willing to support her husband, enabling him to spend all his time working for his cause. Three years later Randolph and a friend named Chandler Owen, who shared his concerns, founded the *Messenger*, a labor newspaper that claimed to be "the only radical Negro Magazine in America."

During the next six years, Randolph and Owen started more than six political and trade unions. Trade unions were associations of workers, such as truck drivers or waiters, who shared the same occupation. Since the late 1800s many American workers had been organizing into unions to fight for shorter hours and other improved working conditions. But none of the unions that Randolph and Owen started were successful. The main obstacles Randolph and Owen encountered were a lack of money and a lack of interest. It was a time when many blacks were so downtrodden that they did not feel anything could be done to improve their situation.

By 1925, however, black railroad porters were beginning to feel they could do something about their condition if they could organize a trade union. They asked Randolph for help. The porters worked on sleeping cars invented by George Pullman. During the day the cars looked like regular coaches, but at night the seat backs could be pushed down to form a straight platform over which mattresses were laid. Pullman deliberately chose ex-slaves as porters. He hired only whites as engineers, conductors, firemen, cooks, and waiters. The Pullman porters served food, made up the beds, and generally saw to the needs of the passengers.

Pullman Company rules about the behavior of porters were very strict. They were supposed to be "Ambassadors of Hospitality," and they were. The porters prided themselves on their appearance and on their service. Many young college-educated black men became porters because there were no other jobs open to them.

But the job was not easy. The Pullman Company decided what the porters' working conditions would be and how much they would be paid—the workers had no input or influence. They worked long hours and got little sleep. There was no provision for a pension plan, and no overtime pay. The porters wanted to organize to fight for their rights.

By the end of World War I organized labor had made great strides in the United States. But the Pullman Company remained firmly against unions. Finally, with the Transportation Act of 1920, Congress passed a law requiring railroad companies to negotiate with unions. The white Pullman conductors organized the Order of Sleeping Car Conductors, and the Pullman Company recognized that union. Other unions were formed and recognized. The black porters hoped to be included in one of the railroad brotherhoods, but in all cases they were denied membership. In 1925 they approached A. Philip Randolph and asked him to help them organize on their own.

Randolph had never been a Pullman porter, nor had he held any other type of railroad job. When he was first approached by the porters, he was reluctant to take on a task that he knew might take years to accomplish. But he eventually agreed, saying simply, "It was a job somebody had to do." He had no idea just how many years of his life it would take to do that job.

On August 25, 1925, Randolph held an organizing meeting of the Brotherhood of Sleeping Car Porters (BSCP) at the Harlem Elks Lodge in New York City. He then began traveling around the country trying to attract membership to the union. This was a difficult job, for the majority of blacks disapproved of unions. Black clergymen and politicians spoke out against the Brotherhood, and a Pullman porter who joined the union faced criticism in his community.

The Pullman Company took advantage of this feeling in the

black community and tried to discredit the Brotherhood further by firing porters who belonged to the union, paying black politicians to speak out against the union, and paying black newspaper publishers to write editorials against the union.

In 1934, after nine years of combatting prejudice from both the white and black communities, Randolph managed to get the Brotherhood admitted to the American Federation of Labor (AFL), an otherwise all-white group of unions. The BSCP was the first all-black union to achieve this status, and it was due to Randolph's unflagging determination and character. That same year he accompanied other labor leaders to meet with President Franklin D. Roosevelt. He then appeared before a congressional committee to plead that porters be included under railroad labor law. He persuaded Congress to amend the rail act, and sleeping car porters and dining car employees were written into the Railway Labor Act of 1934.

Still, the Pullman Company resisted official recognition of the BSCP for another three years. But finally, after months of delicate negotiation, the Pullman Company signed its first labor contract with the Brotherhood of Sleeping Car Porters. It had taken twelve long years for the BSCP to succeed, and it was a victory over far more than the Pullman Company. It was a victory for black rights in general. As Randolph said, "There was no group of Negroes in America who constituted the key to unlocking the door of a nation-wide struggle for Negro rights as [much as] the porters."

After he achieved the formal recognition of his BSCP, Randolph decided to try to build on that victory. He was now one of the most respected and powerful black leaders in the country. During his years as president of the BSCP he had become more and more convinced that the roots of social and political freedom lay in economic freedom. He never failed to sound the call for equality in the workplace. He believed that it was fundamental to black equal rights. And in his union he had a membership that carried his call across the nation. Members of the BSCP were uniquely mobile. As they traveled across the country doing their work, they formed a network for the distribution of political thoughts and literature.

World War II broke out in Europe in the late 1930s, and U.S. defense industries geared up to help their European allies. By early 1941 there was a very real possibility that the United States itself would enter the war, which would mean that even more jobs would be created in the defense industries. It would also mean lifting millions of unemployed workers out of the Great Depression that had afflicted the nation throughout the 1930s. During that time many businesses had failed, leaving workers without jobs. As "last hired and first fired," blacks had suffered especially. Thousands of black workers were out of work, and Randolph wanted to make sure they got some of those defense jobs. He knew they would not get them without political pressure, because the defense industries had a policy of openly discriminating against blacks.

To call attention to this issue, Randolph developed his first plan for a march on Washington. A massive demonstration in the nation's capital would, he hoped, put pressure on President Roosevelt to order an end to discrimination in the factories that made war materials. He began to talk up the idea, and with the BSCP membership behind him, the word got out quickly.

Randolph also hired a young man named Bayard Rustin to help spread the word. Rustin, twenty-three years younger than Randolph, had also attended City College and become a political activist there. At that time Rustin was a member of the Young Communist League. Communism, a revolutionary means of achieving socialism, was embodied in the Soviet Union. Established after the Russian Revolution of 1917, the Union of Soviet Socialist Republics was ruled by one party, the Communist party. The government owned all means of production and distribution. Religion was officially banned, for no institution was to be in competition with the state for the loyalty of its people.

Communists advocated the equality of all peoples, without regard to race, and many young people in the United States at the time, black and white, were sympathetic to it. There were Young Communist League branches on several U.S. college campuses, particularly in the cities.

Randolph did not approve of this more radical form of socialism, but he and Rustin did share the conviction that the black condition in America was part of a larger class struggle and that racism had economic roots.

Randolph asked Rustin to establish a youth division of the March on Washington. He wanted to organize young people as well as adults to fight for black rights. Rustin added this new task to the work he was already doing for the Young Communist League, promoting the march at meetings of various black, labor, and pacifist (antiwar) organizations.

As more and more local March on Washington committees

sprang up around the country, the pressure on President Roosevelt mounted. On June 20, 1941, just two weeks before the scheduled march, he signed Executive Order 8802 banning discrimination in the war industries and establishing the Fair Employment Practices Commission to hear grievances from blacks who felt they were being discriminated against.

In response A. Philip Randolph canceled plans for the demonstration in the nation's capital. While some people doubted that Randolph would have been able to pull off the march, they could not doubt the results of his plan. Thousands of jobs were opened to blacks through Randolph's efforts.

Several years later, after World War II ended, Randolph was instrumental in bringing about another executive order. He had long believed that segregation in the armed forces was wrong. Black soldiers served their country well and bravely during World War II, but segregation had excluded them from high-paying officer positions and barred them from training programs in skills they would need for employment in civilian life. He formed the Committee Against Segregation in the Armed Forces and launched a campaign for integration. Randolph visited President Harry S Truman to discuss the ending of segregation. In 1948, out of respect for Randolph as well as from his own convictions, Truman signed Executive Order 9981 banning segregation in the armed forces.

Thousands of black soldiers had fought for America in World War II. When the war was over and they returned home, they were greeted by the same old segregation and discrimination, and they resented their lack of equality even more than before. Some whites also began to feel that segregation had no place in postwar America. The civil rights movement gained new impetus.

In 1954, following years of effort in the courts by lawyers working for the NAACP, the Supreme Court ruled that segregated public schools were unconstitutional. The Supreme Court's decision in the case of *Brown v. Topeka Board of Education* was a landmark. It gave black Americans new hope that segregation could be ended in other areas of their lives as well.

On December 1, 1955, Rosa Parks, a black seamstress, was arrested for refusing to give up her seat to a white man on a bus in

**Rosa Parks**

Montgomery, Alabama. Her arrest for disobeying the city's segregation laws angered the black community. Local black leaders called for a boycott of the buses. They formed an organization called the Montgomery Improvement Association (MIA) and elected as its president a young minister, Martin Luther King, Jr.

Dr. King had just moved to Montgomery to take up the pastorship of the Dexter Avenue Baptist Church. He was not sure he had the time to devote to the MIA, but he also did not feel he could refuse the position. He realized that this was an opportunity for him to put into practice the ideas about nonviolent social protest he had read about while in college.

In India, Mohandas K. Gandhi had led a movement, beginning in 1915, to win independence from Great Britain through nonviolent protest. He had disobeyed British laws, led demonstrations, and frequently been jailed. Over the years he had attracted the support of the majority of Indians, and by the 1940s world opinion had turned against the British, who finally granted independence to India in 1947.

King believed that nonviolent methods were the only way American blacks could win the full rights of citizenship. Randolph agreed with King and sent Bayard Rustin to Montgomery to help him.

As president of the MIA, King urged black Montgomeryites to stay off the city buses. If whites reacted with violence, the boycotters should not fight back. To aid blacks in the boycott, the MIA organized car pools and arranged for black taxi drivers to drive blacks to work. King and Mrs. Parks gave speeches to raise money to buy station wagons to transport more workers.

The boycott lasted more than a year. The bus company had to stop operating the buses because there were so few riders. Still, the city of Montgomery would not change its segregation laws. The MIA took the case to the U.S. Supreme Court. Only when the court ruled that segregation on public transportation was unconstitutional did the city back down. And only after the city agreed to slight changes in the system of bus seating did the boycott end.

After the success of the boycott, Rustin helped King establish the Southern Christian Leadership Conference (SCLC) to build on that achievement. King and other SCLC founders believed that the time had come to use the tactics of mass protest to fight for equal rights for black people. In 1957, to kick off its campaign, the SCLC decided to hold a Prayer Pilgrimage for Freedom in Washington, D.C.

The SCLC asked other organizations to join the pilgrimage. More than seventy representatives of various groups attended the first organizing meeting. A. Philip Randolph agreed to put his Brotherhood of Sleeping Car Porters behind the effort. He also suggested that Bayard Rustin organize the event, and his suggestion was accepted. Thus, Randolph and Rustin became involved in yet another March on Washington, and this one took place as planned.

The Prayer Pilgrimage was held on May 17, 1957, the third anniversary of the Supreme Court decision in *Brown v. Topeka Board of Education*. Predictions had been for a turnout of 50,000 to 75,000 people, but the actual number was between 15,000 and 25,000. There were many different speakers, King among them. His "Give

Us the Ballot" speech was his first to the nation, and it received the most enthusiastic ovation of any that day.

That same year President Dwight D. Eisenhower introduced the first civil rights act since the Reconstruction period. Congress approved it. But although it provided for far-reaching rights for blacks, it had no "teeth"—no provisions for enforcement, for making sure it was obeyed. It did not bring relief to blacks, and the movement to demand civil rights through protest continued.

Over the next few years, the direct-action civil rights movement in the South diverged from the philosophy that Randolph and Rustin held dear. Spurred by the Student Nonviolent Coordinating Committee (SNCC, usually pronounced "Snick"), formed in 1960 by black and white college students, the civil rights movement adopted different tactics. The new idea was to provoke white authorities so that they would react violently—and they did. There were hundreds of arrests and beatings of civil rights workers. The violence did bring more sympathy for the civil rights movement, but at a great price.

Then, too, the civil rights movement seemed to move away from the economic goals that Randolph continued to feel were the most important. He could cite plenty of statistics to prove his concern. Black unemployment was more than double that of whites, while the average income of a black family was about half that of the average white family. But instead of demanding jobs, which Randolph believed would lead to more integration, the movement concentrated on demanding voting rights.

By 1962, Randolph felt very much out of the mainstream of

history. He did not like sitting on the sidelines; he wanted to get back into the thick of things. In the fall of 1962 he suggested to Rustin another March on Washington. This one would be called the Emancipation March for Jobs, and it would take place on January 1, 1963, to mark the one-hundred-year anniversary of the Emancipation Proclamation, which had freed the slaves.

But the idea did not interest the major civil rights leaders, so Randolph and Rustin changed the name of the proposed march to the March on Washington for Jobs and Freedom. They included in its goals the breaking down of racial barriers in a wide range of areas.

Martin Luther King, Jr., and his SCLC still were not very interested. They were busy planning an all-out campaign against segregation in Birmingham, Alabama, the most segregated city in that state. Bombings of black churches and of the homes of black activists there, including fifty in the past year alone, had earned the city the nickname "Bombingham."

In strategy sessions, leaders of the SCLC decided to target segregated downtown stores with marches and boycotts. They expected to provoke Sheriff Eugene "Bull" Connor to react violently. Connor was well known as a man who would immediately crush any movement for black equality. The SCLC wanted to use Connor to show the nation just how brutal segregation really was.

When Birmingham's black adults did not demonstrate in the mass numbers the SCLC had expected, members of the SCLC recruited black high school students. It was the first time large numbers of black youth had participated in demonstrations. Connor

Birmingham police set dogs on black demonstrators, 1963.

responded by setting dogs on the young people, and firemen attacked them with powerful hoses. After witnessing the attacks on their children, black adults joined the campaign by the thousands. They were arrested and put in jail. In the end, the campaign succeeded in integrating many areas of life in Birmingham. But again, the cost was enormous.

The violent events in Birmingham seemed to spur blacks across the country to action: Demonstrations and marches by the hundreds were being planned. And in the mind of the American public, King and the SCLC were now in the forefront of the direct-action civil rights movement.

Randolph believed that a basic change was occurring in the movement. He predicted that the battle against racism would soon move north: "The Negro masses . . . are going to move. . . . And if Negro leadership does not move rapidly or effectively enough, they will take it into their own hands and move anyhow."

Randolph also believed that the civil rights movement as it was then known was nearing its end. He firmly believed that laws guaranteeing basic civil rights to blacks would be passed over the next few years and that there would be no more need for demonstrations for the right to vote, or to eat in white restaurants, or for other such issues. But these laws would be merely legal victories. The hard period was to follow, for unless blacks could work at jobs to improve their economic condition, they could never really exercise their new legal freedoms.

That new struggle would call for the civil rights organizations to work together as they never had before. He viewed his proposed

March on Washington as a great protest march and as an important cooperative effort of all the major civil rights organizations. If they could effectively join forces in this effort, perhaps they could do it again in the future.

But getting the leaders of all the major organizations to agree to the march was no small challenge.

# CHAPTER 3

# TO MARCH OR
# NOT TO MARCH

**B**efore Randolph could arrange any formal meeting among the civil rights leaders, the Kennedy administration took steps both to stop the racial violence in the South and to make the proposed March on Washington unnecessary. President John F. Kennedy and his brother, Attorney General Robert F. Kennedy, were growing more and more concerned about the violent turn the civil rights movement had taken. The marches and demonstrations, and the bitter white resistance, were creating great unrest across the nation.

In some ways, violent campaigns such as the one in Birmingham had had the same effect on the president as they had on nonracist whites in the rest of the country. They made him understand the brutality of segregation. In fact, the violence in Birmingham and in Jackson, Mississippi, where the NAACP was leading a campaign to desegregate local stores, businesses, and public facilities, spurred Kennedy to make his strongest public statement about black rights up to that time. On June 11, 1963, he went on television to say:

We are confronted primarily with a moral issue. It is as old as the Scriptures and as clear as the American Constitution. The heart of the question is whether all Americans are afforded equal rights and equal opportunities; whether we are going to treat our fellow Americans as we want to be treated. If an American because his skin is dark cannot eat lunch in a restaurant open to the public, if he cannot send his children to the best public school available, if he cannot vote for the public officials who represent him, if in short he cannot enjoy the full and free life which all of us want, then who among us would be content to have the color of his skin changed and stand in his place? Who among us would then be content with the counsels of patience and delay?

The following evening, Medgar Evers was assassinated in front of his home in Jackson, Mississippi. An NAACP field secretary, Evers had been in the forefront of the organization's recent boycotts, demonstrations, and voter registration drives in Mississippi. His accused killer, Byron de la Beckwith, was tried twice for the crime, but both times mistrials were declared. New evidence uncovered in 1991 made yet another trial a possibility. Evers's death at the hands of white racists seemed to underscore the urgency in the president's speech.

Martin Luther King, Jr., believed Kennedy's speech was a direct response to Birmingham. It was proof to him that the tactics of confrontation used in Birmingham worked. He thought the time was right to stage a mass demonstration in Washington, D.C., to pressure the president into signing an executive order declaring segregation

**President John F. Kennedy**

illegal. He knew that such a tactic had worked for A. Philip Randolph back in the 1940s; he also knew that Randolph had been talking about a mass demonstration in the capital, and he had already called Randolph to discuss it.

Randolph had been delighted to hear from King. So far he'd had little success in interesting the leaders of the two oldest and wealthiest civil rights organizations, the NAACP and the National Urban League, in the march. Both Roy Wilkins of the NAACP and Whitney Young of the Urban League were concerned that taking part in such an open protest would damage the close relationships they had developed over the years with many federal officials and members of Congress, as well as with liberal whites. Their concern was similar to that of Walter Reuther, the president of the powerful, mostly white United Auto Workers (UAW). He was sympathetic to the idea of a march on Washington for jobs but did not want to damage his carefully cultivated friendships in Washington. Randolph also knew that the president was playing on those fears, calling on important friends of the civil rights and labor movements to help stop the march. One was Senator Hubert H. Humphrey, Democratic senator from Minnesota, whom Randolph held in high regard. Another was the powerful white labor leader George Meany. Both these leaders had great respect for Randolph, and when they realized he was committed to the march, they did not try to pressure him into backing down. Randolph was not sure what influences were being brought to bear on Wilkins and Young. He hoped that once they learned that King supported the proposed march, they would feel they had to participate or face the prospect of being left behind.

On June 19 President Kennedy introduced a new civil rights bill to Congress. It would be much stronger than the 1957 Civil Rights Act, with new provisions to help guarantee blacks the right to vote and to use public accommodations, such as hotels, restaurants, and places of amusement. More important, it contained provisions to make sure the bill would be enforced: Federal funds to states and institutions could be cut off and the Department of Justice could sue those who did not comply; the Census Bureau could gather voting statistics by race. It was the strongest civil rights bill yet proposed by a twentieth-century president. The bill was a response to Birmingham; it was also a response to the proposed March on Washington. With such an important bill before Congress, Kennedy hoped the march would be canceled.

But his introduction of the bill had the opposite effect—it gave momentum to the march. On June 20, one day after Kennedy introduced the bill, Martin Luther King, Jr., spoke at a meeting of the Alabama Christian Movement for Human Rights. He talked about the upcoming march and about how it would put pressure on Congress to pass Kennedy's civil rights bill. It was his first public statement in support of the march.

Randolph wasted no time before exploiting King's statement. On June 21, on Randolph's instructions, Cleveland Robinson, a New York City labor leader, called a press conference and officially announced the march to the New York press.

Now it was Kennedy's turn to act quickly. He called the major civil rights and labor leaders together for a meeting at the White House to ask that they cancel the march. They arrived at the White

House on June 22, 1963. In the Cabinet Room the invited guests—including A. Philip Randolph, Martin Luther King, Jr., Roy Wilkins, Whitney Young, James Farmer of CORE, and Walter Reuther—took seats around the president's table. Vice President Lyndon B. Johnson also took a seat at the table. Attorney General Robert F. Kennedy sat in a chair apart from the group, holding one of his little daughters in his lap.

President Kennedy addressed the group, explaining that his civil rights bill faced an uphill battle in Congress. He talked about the Southern members of Congress who were threatening to filibuster—they were ready to talk for days or weeks on end to prevent the bill from coming to a vote. He spoke of the most recent national public opinion poll, showing that his popularity had tumbled in the few days since he had introduced the bill. He said he might lose the next presidential election over civil rights, but that he didn't care. He was committed to the cause. But he wanted success in Congress, not a "big show in the Capital."

Everyone in the room knew that Randolph's last march on Washington had been canceled after President Roosevelt had introduced his executive order banning discrimination in the war industries. They also knew that the Kennedy administration hoped that the president's civil rights bill would make the upcoming march unnecessary.

Randolph spoke first, explaining that the situations were different. Blacks were already demonstrating in the streets, he pointed out, and rightly so. A peaceful demonstration in the nation's capital would show the strength of their numbers and their conviction that their cause was just.

Vice President Johnson argued that the way to get members of Congress to pass the bill was to make private agreements with them, to deal in the Capitol hallways. Any other tactic might backfire and set Congress firmly against the bill.

King supported Randolph, adding that the march would dramatize the civil rights issue in a positive way. Farmer seconded King. Wilkins and Young did not commit themselves either way; nor did Walter Reuther. The meeting ended with no one's having been persuaded to change his position—at least not officially. But the Kennedys' attempt to stop the march accomplished one thing: It galvanized the labor and civil rights leaders and convinced them that the march must be held.

Walter Reuther invited everyone to a lunch and strategy session at his hotel suite. There they argued over the future strategy of the civil rights movement. King wanted to continue using the tactics of confrontation, using the Birmingham campaign as a model. Wilkins wanted to work quietly, persuading members of Congress to back new civil rights legislation. The two approaches were diametrically opposed. Later Wilkins would write in his autobiography, *Standing Fast*, "Randolph's march for jobs offered us a perfect compromise. We all adopted it, broadening its purpose to back the civil rights bill. The March on Washington was on."

Because of other commitments, the leaders could not meet until early July to begin organizing the march in earnest. Meanwhile, others were working against the march in their own ways. Many political and business leaders feared that the march would turn violent and cause further unrest and chaos. The economy and the world image of the United States would suffer. The press took up this criticism, saying it was "social dynamite" for so many people to descend on the capital. Such a mob would be impossible to control. Violence would be unavoidable, and it would erase many of the gains the civil rights movement had made.

Some in the press reported that there was not much interest in the march anyway and so it was unlikely that many people would show up.

The most determined critics of the march used what at the time was a very powerful weapon—the charge that the march was a communist plot. The year 1963 was not very far from the 1950s, when fears of communism had put the nation in turmoil. Suspicion that the Soviet Union and its allies were infiltrating the United States and planning to take over its government had caused those who had been even indirectly associated with communist organizations to fear for their jobs and even their safety. Hollywood directors and movie stars, radio personalities, and other celebrities, as well as many people in other less public professions, had been "blacklisted" as suspected communists and been unable to get work.

J. Edgar Hoover, the director of the Federal Bureau of Investigation (FBI) from 1924 to 1972, believed that "Reds," as communists were called, were everywhere. He tried to convince Attorney General Robert Kennedy that Martin Luther King, Jr., was a communist. As evidence, he pointed to a 1957 speech that King had given at the Highlander Folk School, a school in Tennessee that had been established to help workers learn how to fight for their rights. When Kennedy said that one speech was not proof, Hoover said he could prove that some of King's major supporters were communists.

It was true that, mostly many years earlier, some of King's supporters had supported communist causes—most notably Stanley Levison, a New York lawyer and real estate investor, and Jack O'Dell, a young black assistant to Levison who worked in the SCLC's New York office. Most of the major civil rights organizations had received help and money from people who had also helped communist and socialist organizations. Bayard Rustin had been a member of the Young Communist League back in the 1930s.

Although Robert Kennedy disliked Hoover and believed he was overly concerned about communism, he did authorize Hoover to order wiretaps on the telephones of King and some of his supporters. Hoover then ordered one of the most extensive and sordid campaigns to destroy a man in the history of the agency. FBI agents bugged King's telephone and hotel rooms, as well as those of his associates. The information gathered from those wiretaps and listening devices was used not just to identify suspected communists among King's supporters, but later to discredit King himself. From 1963 until King's assassination in 1968, J. Edgar Hoover was obsessed with bringing about King's downfall, and he used blackmail, threats, and every underhanded tactic possible to try to destroy King.

Both Kennedys worried that the connection between communism and the March on Washington would be used by those who were against the march. They were right. At a special joint press conference, Alabama Governor George Wallace and Mississippi Governor Ross Barnett displayed a huge photograph of King making his 1957 speech at the Highlander Folk School, which they called a

"Communist training school." Barnett went further. His charges made headlines in *The New York Times*: "Barnett Charges Kennedys Assist Red Racial Plot."

President Kennedy personally asked King to disassociate himself from Levison and O'Dell, and King reluctantly did so. The civil rights leaders were trying to compromise with Kennedy. In return, when Kennedy realized they were determined to go through with the march, he no longer tried to stop it. If he had, the tone of the march would have been much more confrontational than it was.

Kennedy also took steps to repudiate the charges that the march was somehow communist inspired. On July 17 he called a news conference at which he stated that recent government investigations had shown that none of the civil rights leaders were communists and that none of the civil rights demonstrations were communist inspired.

"I will look forward to being here," he said, referring to the capital on the day of the march. "Members of Congress will be here." He urged any citizens who wanted to come to Washington to express their right of petition to do so.

# CHAPTER 4

# THE BIG SIX,
# AND THE TOP TEN

The march was on. But the real planning had not even begun. All the civil rights organizations and their leaders shared many common goals but disagreed on which goals were most important and on how to achieve them, competing with one another for members, money, and power. Their leaders had healthy egos and followers who were protective of their own particular turf. Although the leaders and organizations had worked with one another off and on, attempts at cooperation had rarely been successful, so A. Philip Randolph and Bayard Rustin felt pleased when they managed to get about fifteen people together for a meeting to talk about the march.

The people who gathered at the planning meeting at the Roosevelt Hotel in New York on July 2, 1963, included several representatives from most of the major civil rights organizations. But then Roy Wilkins arrived. He had been executive director of the NAACP since 1955. On arrival, he took one look at the large table and fifteen or so place settings and announced that this would never

**Roy Wilkins**

do. Taylor Branch, in *Parting the Waters,* his history of the civil rights movement, described what happened next:

> He had come for a chiefs-only meeting, he said, and began literally to tap the men on the shoulders, saying "This one stays. This one goes." A. Philip Randolph could stay, but not Rustin, who had come as his deputy. Among the others Wilkins marked for ejection were Fred Shuttlesworth [of the SCLC], James Forman [executive director of SNCC], Norman Hill of CORE, and Cleveland Robinson, the New York labor leader who had helped subsidize the march preparations by giving Bayard Rustin a union office and a stipend. Wilkins cut through the group like a scythe. It was no small tribute to his stature that he could command obedience from such people as Shuttlesworth and Forman, who had come great distances for the summit meeting but soon retreated sullenly into the hallway. . . . Grumbling furiously among themselves, some of the expelled ones said this power play by Wilkins surely foretold an effort to scuttle the entire march.

Once Wilkins had finished, six were left, the so-called "Big Six" of the March on Washington: A. Philip Randolph, Roy Wilkins, Whitney M. Young, Jr., James Farmer, Martin Luther King, Jr., and John Lewis. The only leader who was not head of a major civil rights organization was Randolph. In addition to being the prime mover behind the march, he represented the Brotherhood of Sleeping Car Porters and, through his other connections with major unions, organized labor in general. When he acted for civil rights, however, he acted as an individual, not as a labor advocate. He was the oldest member of the group.

**Roy Wilkins** was next in age. He was born in St. Louis, Missouri, in 1901. He grew up in St. Paul, Minnesota, and was graduated from the University of Minnesota. He worked as a newspaper reporter with the *Kansas City Call*, a black weekly, before joining the NAACP in 1931 as an assistant to Walter White, who was then the executive director. By 1963 he was a veteran civil rights leader, and he had shown great skill in understanding and using the mechanics of power in Washington, D.C. He was able to get action when others failed and was known as a master strategist.

The NAACP, the oldest black civil rights organization, was founded in 1909 on the one hundredth anniversary of the birth of Abraham Lincoln. The purpose of the NAACP was to achieve, by peaceful and lawful means, equal citizenship rights for all Americans. The organization worked to eliminate segregation in housing, employment, public accommodations, schools, voting, the courts, transportation, and recreation. Beginning in the 1930s the NAACP decided to concentrate on ending segregation through legal challenges in the courts. It was NAACP attorneys like Wiley Branton and Thurgood Marshall who led the legal fight against "separate but equal" public schools. Their efforts had resulted in a major victory when the Supreme Court declared in the case of *Brown v. Topeka Board of Education* in 1954 that separate schools were not equal.

In 1963, at the time of the meeting, the NAACP was still pursuing its cause largely through the courts. Wilkins complained that the other civil rights organizations stirred up trouble and then depended on NAACP attorneys and NAACP money to get them out of it.

**Whitney Young**

**Whitney M. Young, Jr.,** representing the National Urban League, was a large man, six feet tall. He was a take-charge kind of person, and the others sometimes referred to him as the "chairman of the board." He had been executive director of the National Urban League since 1961.

Born in Lincoln Ridge, Kentucky, in 1921, Young grew up on the campus of Lincoln Institute, where his father was a teacher and later president. He was graduated from Kentucky State College in 1941 and served in the U.S. Army with a black road construction company. He then returned to school and earned a degree in social work from the University of Minnesota. As a college teacher he was soon active in the work of the Urban League, first in St. Paul, Minnesota, then in Omaha, Nebraska. He served as dean of the Atlanta University School of Social Work from 1954 until 1960, when he took the post of executive director of the Urban League.

The National Urban League was founded in 1910, just a year after the NAACP began. Its stated purpose was to further the economic progress of blacks, especially in the cities, as its name suggests. Like the NAACP, the Urban League was founded by whites and blacks and boasted a large dues-paying membership. The Urban League was the wealthiest and one of the most effective civil rights organizations. It operated training programs, helped find jobs, and aided in health, education, and housing, especially for blacks from the South, newly arrived in Northern cities.

———

**James Farmer** was the executive director of the Congress of Racial Equality (CORE). Born in Marshall, Texas, in 1920, he was the son of a college professor who was the nation's first black to earn a doctoral degree. Farmer earned a degree in chemistry from Wiley College at the age of eighteen and then earned a divinity degree from Howard University, although he was never ordained a minister. In 1942, while doing further graduate work at the University of Chicago, he founded CORE, and that became his major work.

The first black protest organization to use the techniques of non-

**James Farmer**

violent protest and passive resistance, CORE pioneered the sit-in and first used it in 1943 to integrate a local restaurant in Chicago. More willing to confront the white power structure directly than were the NAACP or the Urban League, CORE also started the Freedom Rides in 1961. Following a Supreme Court decision that interstate transportation facilities could not be segregated, CORE decided to test whether or not that ruling was being obeyed. The Freedom Riders were groups of blacks and whites who rode inter-state buses into the South and then entered bus terminal restaurants and waiting rooms to see if blacks and whites had equal access. They were attacked by mobs in places such as Birmingham and Montgomery, Alabama, and some were severely beaten. In Jackson, Mississippi, and elsewhere they were arrested and jailed. Other organizations joined CORE in the Freedom Rides at first, but after so much violence the others dropped out.

In 1963, Farmer was in his early forties and still in the thick of civil rights work. Although most of the Freedom Riders were younger, he had joined them on those dangerous trips into the South and had been arrested and jailed on one of them in 1961.

————

**Dr. Martin Luther King, Jr.,** was still the leader of the Southern Christian Leadership Conference. He was born in 1929 in Atlanta, Georgia, the son of a Baptist minister with a large black congregation. King attended Morehouse College in Atlanta, Crozier Theological Seminary in Pennsylvania, and Boston University Divinity School, where he earned his doctorate in philosophy. He then accepted the pastorate of the Dexter Avenue Baptist Church in Montgomery, Alabama. He and his wife, Coretta Scott King, had been in Montgomery for only about a year when on December 1, 1955, Rosa Parks was arrested for refusing to give up her bus seat to a white man.

The Montgomery bus boycott that followed the arrest of Rosa Parks brought Martin Luther King, Jr., national fame and proved that nonviolent mass protest was an effective tool for winning civil rights. King formed the Southern Christian Leadership Conference to use the tactic of nonviolence to bring about change in other areas of southern black life.

SCLC's 1957 Prayer Pilgrimage had been planned to kick off a major voting rights campaign. But the SCLC could not seem to attract the support it needed.

In 1960, black college students in Greensboro, North Carolina, guided and advised by CORE, began sit-ins at local lunch counters. The movement spread quickly to other black Southern campuses, and soon it was clear that the civil rights movement that had begun with the Montgomery bus boycott was entering a new, activist phase. The SCLC quickly took steps to harness the energy of the students into organized campaigns. King and other SCLC leaders helped found the Student Nonviolent Coordinating Committee (SNCC) in 1960.

In October 1960, King led a group of blacks in an attempt to get lunch service at ten stores in downtown Atlanta, Georgia. Many were arrested, including King. The 1960 presidential election was to take place in November. Vice President Richard M. Nixon was running on the Republican ticket, hoping to succeed outgoing President Eisenhower. The Democratic candidate was a young Massachusetts senator, John F. Kennedy. The SCLC telegraphed both presidential candidates, asking for their help.

Neither candidate wanted to get involved. If they tried to help the SCLC, they might get more black votes, but they risked losing many white votes. Before either replied, all the demonstrators except King were released from jail. The previous spring he had been arrested for driving in Georgia without a Georgia driver's license, although he had his Alabama license with him. He had been fined twenty-five dollars and was given twelve months' probation. The arrest for demonstrating in Atlanta was a violation of his probation,

**43**

Martin Luther King, Jr., is taken to a Georgia courthouse for his hearing on charges of probation violation.

Atlanta authorities said. He was sentenced to six months' hard labor in a state prison.

Such a harsh sentence for what was originally a trumped-up charge caused worldwide comment. It also caused Coretta Scott King to cry in public for the first time. She was present at her husband's sentencing and was afraid he would be in prison when their new baby arrived (she was five months pregnant at the time). John Kennedy decided he could at least call Coretta Scott King and express his sympathy. This act alone won him many black votes.

In the meantime Robert F. Kennedy, who was helping his brother campaign, made an unofficial call to the attorney general of Georgia to say he thought the harsh sentence imposed on King was ridiculous.

King was released, and in November John F. Kennedy won one of the closest presidential elections in history. Just how much the October events affected Kennedy's narrow victory will never be known for sure.

In the summer of 1962 the SCLC planned a massive campaign for integration in Albany, Georgia, but the campaign failed. The Student Nonviolent Coordinating Committee already had workers organizing a voter registration drive there, and SNCC accused King and the SCLC of coming in and stealing all the glory. They could not agree on strategy, and the campaign was disorganized.

It was important for King personally to show that he and the SCLC could run an organized campaign. Thus, when the Reverend Fred Shuttlesworth of Birmingham, Alabama, had suggested a campaign to desegregate the downtown stores of that city, King had agreed. The violence of that campaign had dismayed King. But he had only grown in stature as a result of Birmingham.

Although he was relatively new to the movement, King was already the most famous civil rights leader. In the jockeying for position among the Big Six, King was, according to CORE director James Farmer:

> far and away in the lead. In a sense, it was a battle for media coverage, for along with headlines in print and on the tube came money to fuel more dramatic thrusts for the media to cover. Ever since the Montgomery bus boycott, King had been a magnet to the press. Envy of Dr. King's visibility was inevitable.

The Student Nonviolent Coordinating Committee had begun in 1960 with King as one of its advisers. By late 1962, however, it had moved away from King's idea of peaceful protest and sought a more dynamic role in the movement. But it was not well organized, and its membership was small. By some estimates, the SNCC never had more than two hundred active members. This was partly because many SNCC workers were college students who could participate only during summer and other vacations.

———

**John Lewis** was one of the founders of SNCC and one of the first students to engage in sit-ins and Freedom Rides. At twenty-three, he was by far the youngest among the Big Six. Small in stature, a mild-mannered devout Baptist, he believed wholeheartedly in the civil rights struggle and was ready to put his life on the line for it.

John Lewis (foreground), James Farmer (above left), Ralph Abernathy (above center), and Martin Luther King, Jr., hold a press conference in Montgomery to announce that the SNCC Freedom Rides will continue.

Between 1960 and 1966 he was jailed more than forty times and savagely beaten several times. He became national chairman of SNCC in 1963 and did not appreciate the efforts of the older and more moderate civil rights leaders.

SNCC's organization was somewhat different from that of the other civil rights groups. It had both an executive director, James Forman, and a national chairman, John Lewis. Roy Wilkins chose

Lewis to represent SNCC at march meetings. Since he was so much younger than the others, Lewis and the youthful SNCC were not taken very seriously. They were outside the circle of power.

There were no women among the Big Six leaders of the March on Washington. However, sometimes when people referred to the Big Six, they meant the group of leaders of the largest black organizations in the country. Dorothy Height, president of the National Council of Negro Women, was included, but as a woman she was even further outside the circle of power than young John Lewis.

A native of Richmond, Virginia, Height held a master's degree in social work from New York University and, before becoming the fourth president of the National Council of Negro Women, had served for many years as a member of the organization's board of directors. The male leaders of civil rights organizations treated her with respect but did not accord her equal power.

The civil rights movement's attitude toward women was very much a product of the times. Most women in those days did not hold positions of power, and men would not have tolerated their involvement. Whether in business or politics or in civil rights organizations, women were welcome to help only. They were expected to type, file, answer telephones, and cook, and to do whatever other support work was necessary, but not to participate in major decisions.

The National Council of Negro Women was established in 1935 by the well-known black educator Mary McLeod Bethune. The largest black women's organization, its broad purpose was to achieve equality of opportunity and eliminate prejudice and discrimination based on race, religion, sex, or national origin. Its major work was with the poor, with juvenile delinquents, and with the aged. The council advocated education instead of confrontation and was not an activist organization like the others. It had little to do—officially— with the March on Washington.

A. Philip Randolph had his work cut out for him when he assembled the other five male leaders and tried to get them to agree on the purpose and format of the upcoming march. Roy Wilkins felt that lobbying, or trying to persuade, individual members of Congress would accomplish more than marching. Whitney Young tended to feel that way, too. King, although he was generally quiet in meetings of the Big Six, wanted to apply the confrontational tone of the Birmingham campaign to the march. Both Lewis and Farmer suspected that the march was really an attempt to control them and their organizations. It took all of Randolph's persuasive powers to get the members of the group to agree to cooperate with each other.

When the six got down to business, Randolph began by saying that he had dreamed of a march on Washington for twenty years and that he wanted Bayard Rustin to make it a reality. Roy Wilkins immediately objected. Rustin was a socialist who had once been a member of the Young Communist League; many Americans considered that traitorous. Rustin had refused to join the armed services in World War II because he was a conscientious objector who did not believe in war; many Americans considered conscientious objectors to be traitors. Rustin was also somewhat openly homosexual, and had once been arrested in California for homosexual activity. All this would come out, Wilkins warned, and criticism of Rustin would harm the march.

Young agreed with Wilkins. So did King and Farmer, although they recognized Rustin's organizing skills. Someone suggested that Randolph himself lead the march. Randolph answered that if he did, he would insist upon the right to choose Rustin as his deputy. Wilkins said that was Randolph's right, but that he should expect trouble over Rustin.

As Wilkins had predicted, as soon as word got out that Rustin was the chief march organizer, he was attacked on the floor of the United States Senate. Senator Strom Thurmond of South Carolina denounced the march by denouncing Rustin. Rustin was a draft dodger, a homosexual, and a communist, Thurmond said. Any march that Rustin organized had to be anti-American.

Thurmond's attack made newspaper headlines. Randolph moved quickly to respond, and to his credit, Wilkins did not say "I told you so" to Randolph. Instead, he urged that the march leaders present a united front. Randolph called a press conference at his Harlem office. There, with Wilkins and the other march leaders beside him, he issued a brief statement: "We, the leaders of the March on Washington, have absolute confidence in Bayard Rustin's character and abilities." He then refused to answer any questions about Rustin.

For a time reporters would not let the issue drop. Repeatedly, they asked the leaders about Rustin. But whether the leader was King or Wilkins or Young or someone else, each time the answer was the same: "As Mr. Randolph has said . . ." Eventually, the reporters stopped asking.

In return for the support of the other black leaders on the issue of Rustin, Randolph agreed to open the march leadership to include whites. He had envisioned a march by black people, but Roy Wilkins and Whitney Young wanted a large number of whites involved. For this reason, they invited white religious and labor leaders to participate in the planning of the march.

The Catholic spokesman was Mathew Ahmann, executive director of the National Catholic Conference for Interracial Justice. The Protestant member was Dr. Eugene Carson Blake, vice chairman of the Commission on Race Relations of the National Council of Churches of Christ in America. Rabbi Joachim Prinz, president of the American Jewish Congress, completed the spectrum of the major religious groups in the United States. In addition, Walter Reuther, president of the United Auto Workers, represented the trade union movement. Thus, the Big Six expanded to become part of a new group called the Top Ten.

The Top Ten agreed that the march would be held on August 28. Randolph chose the date, suggesting that the march would give militant black youth a positive way to express themselves in the heat of the summer. The Top Ten also agreed that the march would take place on the Mall and that it would begin at the Washington Monument and end one mile away at the Lincoln Memorial. There, at the monument to the man who had issued the Emancipation Proclamation, the main program would be held. They further agreed that the tone of the march would be positive, with no confrontations or threats of violence. It would be a massive peaceful display of black and white citizens urging justice and equal rights *now.*

**Bayard Rustin**

# CHAPTER 5

# THE PLAN

**B**ayard Rustin was not well known to the general public, but he had been working most of his life for the civil rights cause and had been arrested twenty-two times. He had helped found the Congress of Racial Equality, had participated in CORE's first Freedom Rides in 1947, and had helped found the Southern Christian Leadership Conference. He had traveled to India to study the nonviolent protest movement led by Mohandas K. Gandhi, who had so influenced Martin Luther King, Jr. He was good friends with the leaders of the newly independent African nations. He was responsible for much of the thinking behind the civil rights movement, but he was not considered a black leader and did not wish to be.

Bayard Rustin's greatest skill was in organization, and organizing was one of the things he liked best to do. He had organized a peace walk in England, an anti–atom-bomb march in France, and a rally against anti-Semitism in West Germany. He looked forward to the challenge of organizing the biggest march of his career, and he was going to need all his skills.

Once the Top Ten had met and decided on the plan, he had less than two months to figure out how to move the expected crowd of 100,000 people into and out of the capital in one day and how to make sure that that day went peacefully and comfortably for everyone involved.

He also needed all his skills as a negotiator, for while it would have been easier for him to have made alone all the decisions that were necessary, he knew that the Top Ten, and especially the Big Six, would want to be in on all decisions.

Two days after he was named deputy director of the march, he prepared a memo for Randolph to send to the other organizers. The memo stated that the march would have its organizing headquarters in Harlem. It also stated that all ten cochairmen should have representatives at the headquarters, as all decisions would be made cooperatively. The other leaders agreed, and the planning went on from there.

There were so many things to think about: One big need was for money. The march organizers wanted to bring thousands of unemployed and poor people from across the country to Washington. Rustin calculated that they would need fifteen thousand dollars to transport and house these people. They had to spend money for the printing of press releases informing people about the upcoming march and urging them to take part. They needed to print up instructions for the marchers and signs for them to carry. Rustin estimated that they would need at least ten thousand dollars for printed materials. In addition to planning all the details of the event, march organizers were constantly working to raise more money. Fortunately, money did come in from a variety of sources, and many of the things that were needed, such as blankets, were donated. The NAACP put up ten thousand dollars to get the planning started. The Urban League made a substantial contribution, and so did Walter Reuther, on behalf of the trade union movement. But much more was needed.

A bigger question was how actually to persuade 100,000 people to participate in the march. A lot of publicity was needed in a short period of time. Immediately, they issued a "Call to Americans to Join the March on Washington for Jobs and Freedom" through the black press and various mailing lists supplied by civil rights and labor organizations. It ended with the words: "We call upon you and upon churches, fraternal societies, labor unions, civic groups, youth groups, and professional associations to accelerate the dynamic, nonviolent thrust of the civil rights revolution by joining the March on Washington for Jobs and Freedom."

Transportation was another major concern. The bulk of the marchers had to travel to Washington by bus or train. To encourage too many private cars would be to invite traffic jams. Walter Reuther saw to it that all the trade unions provided their own buses. Some arranged for bus transportation free of charge. Others charged only a small amount to transport the marchers. The large civil rights organizations such as the NAACP and Urban League also provided buses. In most cases they charged adults but let young people ride free.

In order to pay their way on the buses, people raised money in a

*An Appeal to You from*

| | |
|---|---|
| **MATHEW AHMANN** | **JOACHIM PRINZ** |
| **EUGENE CARSON BLAKE** | **A. PHILIP RANDOLPH** |
| **JAMES FARMER** | **WALTER REUTHER** |
| **MARTIN LUTHER KING, JR.** | **ROY WILKINS** |
| **JOHN LEWIS** | **WHITNEY YOUNG** |

# *to MARCH on*
# WASHINGTON
## WEDNESDAY AUGUST 28, 1963

*America faces a crisis . . .*
*Millions of Negroes are denied freedom . . .*
*Millions of citizens, black and white, are unemployed . . .*

*We demand:*
— Meaningful Civil Rights Laws
— Massive Federal Works Program
— Full and Fair Employment
— Decent Housing
— The Right to Vote
— Adequate Integrated Education

In your community, groups are mobilizing for the March. **You can get information on how to go to Washington by calling civil rights organizations, religious organizations, trade unions, fraternal organizations and youth groups.**

*National Office —*

# MARCH ON WASHINGTON
# FOR JOBS AND FREEDOM

**170 West 130 Street**  •  **New York 27**  •  **FI 8-1900**

**Cleveland Robinson**
*Chairman, Administrative Committee*

**Bayard Rustin**
*Deputy Director*

variety of ways. They held fashion shows, house parties, receptions, and even bake sales. A group of unemployed black men in Cleveland, Ohio, raised the thirty-three dollars for their chartered bus tickets by selling shares in their tickets. For one dollar, a person could be represented at the March on Washington by one of the men. Thus, each man went on behalf of thirty-three people.

What was to be done with all the buses once they reached Washington, D.C.? Rustin convinced the authorities to ban street parking in a huge corner of northwest Washington to make room for the buses. He arranged for each bus to have a captain and for each captain to have an envelope of instructions. The instructions told them where the bus was to park, when it was supposed to leave the capital, and where to go for help in locating the bus. He arranged for an information office staffed with people who could transport marchers back to their buses if they could not get there themselves.

Washington's Union Station planned to run dozens of special trains, and the D.C. Transit Company set up a shuttle bus to transport people from the station to the grounds of the Washington Monument.

Ease of communication was critical. Rustin knew that all the march organizers needed to be close to telephones so they could stay in touch with each other. He did not have enough money to pay for the installation of hundreds of telephones, so he went for help to the local telephone company. At first the company was reluctant to help, but Rustin made them consider what would happen if the march dissolved into violence because the march organizers could not communicate with each other. As a result, the telephone company installed hundreds of pay telephones at its own expense.

A large number of these phones would be in an enormous green tent that would serve as the center of march activity. Rustin planned to be in that tent and to have a network of phones and workers located all along the march route from the Lincoln Memorial to the Washington Monument, and also in the parking lots, Union Station, and the airports. That way he could pick up a telephone and call anywhere he needed, and people in those areas could in turn call him if there were any problems.

Food for all the participants was also part of the plan. Rustin expected that most people planning for a long bus trip and a long day would bring food. But he knew he had to provide food for those who did not, and for those who did not bring enough. He arranged for volunteers to make sandwiches and to have inexpensive fruit and beverages available.

Some people would arrive very early, perhaps the night before or in the very early morning. Even though it was late August, the nighttime and early morning hours might be cool. Rustin arranged for the U.S. Army to provide forty thousand blankets for people who might want to sleep.

Although everyone would be urged to leave the District of Columbia when the march was over, a special housing committee was appointed to line up a thousand emergency beds in and around Washington.

There were also issues of health and hygiene. Rustin ordered several thousand portable toilets, to be installed along the march route and on the Mall. Some of these comfort stations were in giant government trucks, with facilities for thirty or forty people. He arranged for twenty-four first-aid stations, each with two doctors, four nurses, two ambulances, and medical supplies. The District of Columbia Health Department and the D.C. Red Cross would staff those stations. The march organizers suggested that a professional nurse be on each bus or train in case of emergencies. Rustin also arranged for twenty-one temporary drinking fountains to be installed. "Order," he later explained, "stemmed from answering people's needs rather than from policing people."

Even though the march would be orderly, there was a need for police. Everyone involved in the planning of the march took seriously the possibility of violence. They were not as worried about the marchers themselves as they were about the Ku Klux Klan or other right-wing groups who might try to disrupt the march.

The FBI took on the job of trying to find out if any such groups were planning counterprotests. That was the only kind of FBI help Rustin wanted. In fact, he did not want any visible presence at the march from the FBI, the National Guard, or the Washington, D.C., police force. He wanted police he could control, so he organized his own force to patrol the march closely.

Rustin's force was made up of professional policemen who volunteered for this duty. The officers would not be in uniform and would not carry weapons, but they would carry handcuffs. Rustin agreed with the British theory that unarmed police were less apt to provoke people to wrongdoing. In fact, he had a black policeman from England come to the United States to help him organize the special March on Washington police force.

In the end, there were two police forces, because Rustin decided to divide them into black and white forces. He later explained,

> We did not want any possibility of any racial friction, where a white person was arresting a black person or a black person was arresting a white person. We also made it clear that if there were black elements that misbehaved along the routes coming in to the city, that normal policemen would operate in their areas; but if there were any assaults by the Ku Klux Klan or any white right-wing groups, that black police would have nothing to do with stopping that, that that would be exclusively in the hands of the Washington police—white—and the FBI—white. . . . In other words, instead of being color blind, to make certain that there was no problem we were going to be color conscious.

The perimeter of the 180-acre demonstration area, and an even wider area around that, would be policed by two thousand Washington, D.C., officers, two thousand National Guardsmen, and two hundred park police. Nearby, four thousand Army and Marine troops would be on call.

All the while Rustin was organizing his own police force, he was taking steps to make sure it would not be needed. He asked that there be no posters or slogans except those provided by the march organizing committee. He met several times with leaders of the Communist party, who planned to send groups to the march. "You are welcome to join us," he told them, "but you must not advertise your own cause." The leaders agreed to carry only official march banners.

Two organizing manuals for the march were printed and distributed to the participants. The first told what the march was about, who the sponsors were, and what its demands were. It also emphasized that everyone was invited to the march except "totalitarian or subversive groups of all persuasions." It listed the publicity literature that was available from march headquarters and urged all organizers and participants to help in spreading the word. It also gave instructions for organizing transportation, sketched out the planned schedule for the day, and asked for financial contributions.

The second organizing manual, released close to march time, reiterated much that was in the first. The sponsors and reasons for the march remained the same. The original eight demands had increased to ten:

1. Comprehensive and effective *civil rights legislation* from the present Congress—without compromise or filibuster—to guarantee all Americans
   - access to all public accommodations
   - decent housing
   - adequate and integrated education
   - the right to vote

2. Withholding of Federal funds from all programs in which discrimination exists.

3. *Desegregation of all school districts in 1963.*

4. Enforcement of the *Fourteenth Amendment*—reducing Congressional representation of states where citizens are disenfranchised.

5. A new *Executive Order* banning discrimination in all housing supported by federal funds.

6. Authority for the Attorney General to institute *injunctive suits* when any constitutional right is violated.

7. A massive federal program to train and place all unemployed workers—Negro and white—in meaningful and dignified jobs at decent wages.

8. A national *minimum wage* act that will give all Americans a decent standard of living. (Government surveys show that anything less than $2.00 an hour fails to do this.)

9. A broadened *Fair Labor Standards Act* to include all areas of employment which are presently excluded.

10. A federal *Fair Employment Practices Act* barring discrimination by federal, state, and municipal governments, and by employers, contractors, employment agencies, and trade unions.

By the time this list of demands was issued, the thinking about the purpose of the march had been refined. Now the march leaders regarded it as a huge lobbying effort. To this end they had invited every member of Congress and the Senate to attend and hear the demands. A section of seats at the Lincoln Memorial had even been reserved for them. The manual asked that no groups schedule separate meetings with their senators or representatives, because that might make it difficult for them to be present at the Lincoln Memorial program.

After emphasizing the need to publicize the march and to raise money for it, the manual concentrated on giving detailed directions—"How Do I Get to Washington?" and "How Do We Leave Washington?" The manual specified which types of organizations could carry identifying banners and made it clear that all slogans carried in the march would be designed exclusively by the National Committee and would be distributed at the Washington Monument.

The manual stated that each bus, train, and plane must have a captain and explained what the duties of a captain were. The manual also explained that the National Committee had its own system of marshalls for captains to call on if needed.

In a section titled "Food, Health, and Sanitation Facilities," the manual suggested that each marcher pack two box meals, one for midday and one for supper. It warned against including things that might spoil, such as mayonnaise or salads, and even provided a list of suggested foods: peanut butter and jelly sandwiches, apples or other fruits, brownies or plain cakes, and soft drinks.

Other advice in this section included: Get a good night's sleep the night before; be kind to your stomach—don't eat or drink the wrong foods in the wrong quantities.

Bayard Rustin and the others on the National Committee had tried to think of everything, in order not just to get all the participants in and out of the capital in an orderly fashion, but also to keep them healthy and content.

Some of the advice in the manual seemed unnecessary. But as Bayard Rustin had learned from experience, "If you want to organize anything, assume that everybody is absolutely stupid. And assume yourself that you're stupid."

# CHAPTER 6

# COUNTDOWN

**A**ll the planning by the march organizing committee was done in the hope that 100,000 people would participate. But throughout July and into August it was not at all clear that the march would be well attended.

By early August the idea of the march started to catch on. More and more groups wrote to Rustin to inform him that they planned to participate—groups like the Farband–Labor Zionist Order based in New York and the Japanese American Citizens League based in Washington, D.C.

But one large organization refused officially to support the march, to the great disappointment of A. Philip Randolph. In the middle of August, the executive council of the AFL-CIO, which was made up of nearly all the major labor unions, voted to withhold its support. The council gave as its reasons the fear that the march might anger more members of Congress than it would influence, and that if violence should occur the AFL-CIO might be blamed if it were an official sponsor.

But Randolph knew that there was another, unspoken reason: Many of the affiliated unions had large Southern white memberships or planned to do more organizing in the South in the future. They did not want to alienate Southern whites. Other unions had few black members, and the majority of their white members opposed the march.

Randolph had first proposed the march at the February meeting of the AFL-CIO executive council, and he had been trying ever since to get its support. When he did not get it, he asked the council to contribute to transportation costs for the march, but it refused.

The council did make it clear that any of its affiliated unions could take part in the march without violating the official policies of the Federation. But this concession was unavoidable since Walter Reuther of the AFL-CIO affiliated United Auto Workers was one of the Top Ten, and since a number of unions had already acted in support of the march. Some unions disaffiliated because of the AFL's vote.

Local branches of the International Ladies Garment Workers Union (ILGWU) in several northeastern cities offered to pay the travel and meal expenses for all members who participated. The ILGWU arranged for special trains out of New York and chartered fifteen buses for their members.

Other unions that planned to participate included the Union of Electrical Workers, the Communication Workers of America, and, of course, A. Philip Randolph's Brotherhood of Sleeping Car Porters.

Many celebrities also announced they would participate: Hollywood stars like Sidney Poitier, Charlton Heston, and Marlon Brando; musical entertainers like Lena Horne, Mahalia Jackson, and Harry Belafonte; the writer James Baldwin, who would fly in from Paris; and the comedian Dick Gregory. Even Josephine Baker sent word that she was coming. Baker, born in the United States in 1906, had spent most of her life in Europe, where she was a star beloved and famous as she could not have been in the United States. She strongly supported the civil rights movement in her native country, and attending the march was her way of showing that support.

Once they realized how many celebrities would be at the march, the organizing committee decided that room ought to be made for them on the program, so the program was divided into two parts. First the entertainers would perform for the crowd at the Washington Monument. Then, after the march to the Lincoln Memorial, the civil rights leaders would give their speeches.

Whenever they had time, Rustin and the other march organizers discussed and refined the program. The first part, at the Washington Monument, made up primarily of entertainers, would allow the marchers to assemble and latecomers to join in. Then everyone would go on the mile-long march along Constitution and Independence avenues to the Lincoln Memorial for a more formal program.

The program, beginning with the National Anthem, would include an invocation by the Very Reverend Patrick O'Boyle, archbishop of the Catholic diocese of Washington, and opening remarks by A. Philip Randolph, the march director. Randolph's remarks would be followed by speeches by the Top Ten, interspersed with musical selections and a tribute to Negro Women Fighters for Freedom presented by Myrlie Evers, widow of the NAACP field director Medgar Evers who had been killed in June. This would be the only part of the program involving women.

Just who would speak when was an issue of some importance to the Top Ten, especially to the leaders of the civil rights organizations. Everyone knew that the first speaker's remarks would be remembered least and the last remembered most. It was decided that John Lewis, the youngest member of the Ten and the representative of SNCC, the youngest organization, would speak first. According to this line of thinking, Roy Wilkins would have spoken last. But he did not want to follow Martin Luther King, Jr. In fact, no one wanted to follow King, for the obvious reason that King was the most charismatic speaker. So King was scheduled to speak last, followed only by closing remarks by Randolph and a benediction by Dr. Benjamin E. Mays, president of Morehouse College in Atlanta. Beginning with Lewis's speech, there would be eight long addresses. Rustin made it his business to ensure that they would not be too long. He didn't want the crowd to get bored, but most of all he wanted everyone out of the capital before nightfall. Most of the leaders were notoriously long-winded, so Rustin informed all speakers that a man with a long hook would yank them from the platform if they spoke longer than seven minutes!

The march organizing committee also decided that all speakers should submit copies of the speeches they intended to give before the march. Copies were distributed to the press, who were expected to cover the march in large numbers, so that they would be able to quote the speeches accurately.

The bigger the planned march became, the more important it was to make sure everything was done to increase efficiency. As August wore on, the march got bigger and bigger. The idea of the march had mushroomed, taking on a life of its own. Financial contributions increased. People sent money with notes saying "I cannot march, but here's a contribution." March headquarters was flooded with notices from people who were planning to participate.

Meanwhile, groups of racist whites such as the American Nazi party, beginning to realize that the march was something to be reckoned with, tried to organize countermarches. The New York branch of the party distributed leaflets urging whites to travel to the capital on August 28 to show white solidarity: "August 28 will be the day that the White Man will sweep away the Black Revolution, as though it never existed. Washangton [sic], D.C., will be the battle ground," read one leaflet distributed in New York.

The FBI kept its eye on such groups, and with the Washington police and the march marshalls, they were ready for them. President Kennedy and the chiefs of the military had devised plans of action that would bring in four thousand troops assembled in the suburbs and fifteen thousand paratroopers at the ready in North Carolina if they were needed.

Some people started for Washington, D.C., well in advance of march day. A group from the Brooklyn, New York, chapter of CORE decided to make the 237-mile trip on foot. They started out from New York on August 15 carrying signs that read We March

From New York City for Freedom. Eighty-two-year-old Jay Hardon rode his bicycle all the way from Dayton, Ohio. Ledger Smith decided to roller-skate the 750 miles from Chicago, wearing a bright-red sash that read Freedom. Twenty-three people, including three whites, chartered a bus from Little Rock, Arkansas. Families and groups of friends piled into vans and cars to travel from as far away as California and Louisiana.

Early Tuesday morning, August 27, three buses pulled away from Milwaukee, Wisconsin. That same morning four busloads left St. Louis. Six buses left Birmingham, Alabama, carrying the Alabama delegation on the twenty-two-hour trip. Later in the day two special trains left Chicago; others pulled out of stations in Pittsburgh and Detroit. Yet another pulled out of Jacksonville, Florida, to make stops in Waycross and Savannah, Georgia, and in Richmond, Virginia. On the West Coast, a chartered plane carrying thirty celebrities took off from Lockheed Airport.

Marchers came from Indiana and Ohio and Delaware, from Vermont and Connecticut and Massachusetts, from Pennsylvania and Georgia and New Jersey, talking about freedom, singing spirituals, and praying.

As estimates of the number of expected marchers increased, so did the fears of the people of Washington, D.C. Many government offices and private businesses decided to close for the day. By Congressional decree, all bars and liquor stores were to be closed on march day. The Washington Senators baseball team postponed two games until the day following the march.

The day before the march saw a frenzy of activity. On the grassy slopes below the Washington Monument, workers were erecting rest tents marked with large red crosses. Lines from speaker systems were being strung through trees to the Washington Monument and Lincoln Memorial. Seven thousand portable toilets, 21 four-faucet drinking fountains, and all the pay telephones were installed. On Independence and Constitution avenues police were putting up No Parking signs. All the preparations seemed to be going ahead on schedule. But the march was about more than military-type preparedness. It was also about people, and it was people who presented some last-minute threats to a pleasant and successful march.

One of these people was Malcolm X, the Black Muslim leader who, in his own way, was as charismatic as Dr. King. The Black Muslims, whose formal name was the Nation of Islam, did not believe in answering white violence with nonviolence, preaching instead self-defense. They argued against integration and urged black self-help and separatism. They cast off their "slave last names," charging that they were the names masters had given to slaves, and took either Muslim names or a simple "X," as Malcolm X, who was born Malcolm Little, had done.

As minister of Muslim Temple Number 7 in New York City, the media capital of the world, Malcolm X had a national pulpit. He was an intelligent, witty man who had single-handedly increased the membership of the Nation of Islam many times over. He preached the beliefs of the Nation of Islam and was often quoted in newspapers and magazines and on television. Many blacks who were not members of the Nation of Islam agreed with what he had to say.

Malcolm X was critical of the march, calling it the "Farce on

Malcolm X

Washington." He charged that the Kennedy administration had been able to make "puppets" of the civil rights leaders and to turn the march into a Kennedy pep rally. He traveled to Washington in order to hold a press conference the night before the march, to denounce it.

In Washington he registered at the Statler-Hilton Hotel and was meeting informally with reporters when word came to him that the civil rights leaders wanted to meet with him. The leaders were very concerned that if he did hold a press conference on August 27, he might persuade some people not to attend the march. They managed to talk him out of holding the planned press conference that day, trying to convince him that he would be going against the entire black community if he spoke out, because the entire black community was united in support of the march. Malcolm X backed down.

He did hold a press conference the next day, during the march, and denounced the demonstrators for "seeking favors" from the "white man's Government." But by then his words could have no effect on the number of people who showed up. And coverage of his press conference was not extensive, since most reporters were covering the march itself.

Bayard Rustin, who knew and liked Malcolm X, understood that in canceling his press conference for August 27, Malcolm too had compromised for the good of the black community. Years later Rustin wrote with great pride about how so many individuals and groups had put their own agendas aside for the good of the march:

> This was a time, and one of those few moments in American history, when there was almost absolute unity within the

black community. I don't know that it ever existed before, and I don't think it will ever exist again. But that occurred. Even the communists who joined the march held only our own posters, which we ourselves distributed."

Meanwhile the scheduled speakers had submitted copies of their prepared speeches to the march organizing committee, and copies were made available to the press table at the Statler-Hilton Hotel, where the Top Ten were staying. Robert F. Kennedy's staff read the speeches and were concerned about the speech to be delivered by SNCC's John Lewis. Worried that its fiery words would inflame crowd emotions at the march, the Kennedy staffers gave the speech to Archbishop Patrick O'Boyle. On Tuesday afternoon, O'Boyle lodged a formal complaint against it.

The speech had been written by committee; SNCC usually worked that way. Various members had added to Lewis's speech, calling attention to outrages that had been committed against SNCC workers, criticizing the Kennedy administration's proposed civil rights bill, and generally taking a very militant tone. James Forman had added lines in which he envisioned a conquest over segregation by the civil rights movement equal to that of the Union forces over the Confederacy in the Civil War, and specifically cited Union general William T. Sherman's "march to the sea," in which his forces burned Atlanta and whatever other cities and towns were in their way: "We will march through the South, through the heart of Dixie, the way Sherman did. We shall pursue our own 'scorched earth' policy and burn Jim Crow to the ground—nonviolently. We shall crack the

South into a thousand pieces and put them back together in the image of democracy."

O'Boyle thought such statements were too militant and too political, and when he discussed the speech and his feelings with Walter Reuther and some of the other white leaders of the march, they agreed. But Lewis defended his statements and refused to back down. The debate over the speech continued as the countdown to march time grew shorter.

In New York City, in the great hall of Riverside Church, a crew of three hundred volunteers from the Church World Service made up eighty thousand bag lunches of cheese sandwiches, apples, and pound cake to be transported to Washington overnight. The District of Columbia brought in water in eight 2,500-gallon tank trucks, five 250-gallon water trailers, and dozens of four-place fire hydrant bubblers. According to the District's public health director, 35,000 people an hour could have a good, long drink of water. Preparations went on until the day before march day turned into March Day itself.

At one thirty A.M. on August 28 the first of 450 chartered buses left the Armory at 143rd Street in Harlem. At two-thirty A.M. on August 28, 80 buses supplied by CORE set out from 125th Street in Harlem, each loaded with tired but excited people wearing comfortable walking shoes and carrying their two lunches. Most had planned to nap on the way to Washington, to be rested for the long day ahead, but the excitement was so great that few could sleep. They did more talking and singing than sleeping.

James Farmer, executive director of CORE, was not on one of these buses. In fact, he would not be at the march. Instead he was in jail in Plaquemine, Louisiana, having been arrested a week or so before the March on Washington for leading a march against police brutality. Both Roy Wilkins of the NAACP and Whitney Young of the Urban League sent telegrams to him there, offering to bail him out and urging him to come to the march. But Farmer declined. Two hundred other marchers had been arrested with him; he did not feel he could leave them. He was the only one of the Top Ten who did not make it to Washington, D.C., that historic day.

Several hours after the CORE buses left Harlem, a special fourteen-car train left New York's Pennsylvania Station for Washington, D.C. The departure of special buses and trains was being repeated in cities across the nation. Two special trains, thirty-seven cars each, carried a delegation from Chicago. One of the trains even had a jazz combo for entertainment. And one of the trains carried perhaps the oldest demonstrator, ninety-four-year-old Samuel Harris.

Other special trains departed from Jacksonville, Florida; Detroit, Michigan; and Philadelphia, Pennsylvania. In all, more than 40 such trains and 2,200 chartered buses delivered people to Washington.

Everyone was in a happy mood. "Good News, Freedom's Coming!" they sang, and "We Shall Overcome."

But everyone was also mindful of the great responsibility to behave with dignity. On the special train out of New York there was hushed silence as ministers on each coach offered prayers: "Help us, O Lord," said one, "not to disgrace ourselves this day. Help us to make this a proud day."

In the meantime, thousands of private cars were on their way to the capital. They carried families and groups of friends, and sometimes groups of strangers who had decided to carpool. They consulted maps so as not to miss the right turns and hoped they would get there in time to find a parking space.

Many celebrities arrived the night before and stayed in hotels. Most other marchers could not afford hotels. Those who arrived late that night or very early the next day slept on the grassy slopes around the Washington Monument, thankful for the blankets the march organizing committee had thought to provide.

As night turned into dawn, the city of Washington stirred and suddenly realized that March Day had finally arrived. Everyone wondered what was in store.

But A. Philip Randolph was already pleased. At a press conference on the eve of the march, he announced that the basic goal of the march had already been won: "It has focused the attention of the country on the problems of human dignity and freedom for Negroes," he said. "It has reached the heart, mind, and conscience of America."

# CHAPTER 7

# MARCH DAY DAWNS

**W**ednesday, August 28, 1963, dawned warm and humid, but the forecast was for a high temperature of 84 degrees, not nearly as hot as it could get in Washington, D.C., in August. The march organizers and participants were glad of that, for intense heat would have been uncomfortable, especially for a crowd that was now estimated at 200,000. A hot day also might have caused tempers to shorten and flare, creating a climate ripe for violence.

The potential for violence was present at the Washington Monument even before dawn. The sun had just reached the top of the 555-foot white spire when George Lincoln Rockwell, head of the American Nazi party, arrived with a group of about fifty followers, mostly young men, and predicted that at least two hundred would be there eventually. He'd had pledges, he said, from some twelve thousand, but he did not expect nearly that many to come.

The police allowed Rockwell and his people to gather off the

grounds of the monument in a grassy area about twenty-five yards square. District of Columbia policemen and Air National Guard Military Police took up posts in and around it.

The Nazis were warned not to make speeches, wear uniforms, or show placards. They had applied for a permit to demonstrate but had been turned down. Representatives of CORE had protested, saying the Nazis had just as much right as anybody else to demonstrate. But the D.C. police were taking no chances.

An hour later about seventy-five followers of Rockwell had gathered. "I'm ashamed of my race," the leader muttered, disappointed with the small turnout. He then ordered his deputy chief,

Karl R. Allen, to speak to them. Allen began: "We are here to protest in a peaceful manner the occupation of the nation's capital with people deadly to the welfare of the country." The police then cut in to remind him that he did not have a permit to speak. When he tried twice more to speak, the police moved in and arrested him. It was the first arrest of March Day.

The Nazi group then left, marching in single file more than a mile to a Potomac bridge, then crossed it to Virginia, where the American Nazi party is headquartered.

In another early-morning incident, an anonymous caller told the police that bombs had been placed at the Washington Monument and Lincoln Memorial. But a search of the two monuments turned up nothing.

Marchers continued to arrive, unaware of either the bomb threat or the Nazi demonstration. By dawn several hundred people had gathered on the grassy slopes near the Washington Monument. By seven A.M. there were an estimated thousand. Rustin and the others had expected more people to have arrived by then. They began to wonder if the projections of 200,000 or more marchers might have been too hopeful.

But people were continuing to arrive by car and bus and plane and train. At Union Station a group from Savannah, Georgia, got off their train and made the station's great hall echo with the song "Which Side Are You On?" Shuttle buses took them to the Washington Monument, where by nine thirty A.M. there were some 40,000 people around the monument, and by eleven A.M. close to 100,000. Reports came in that the highways around the capital were

**Marchers arrive at Union Station.**

clogged with cars, inching along toward the city bumper to bumper. These included a two-hundred car caravan from North Carolina. By ten A.M. the stream of cars was tremendous, and it continued to grow for two more hours.

The second arrest of the day came when a youth from Hyattsville, Maryland, was caught throwing stones at march buses on the Baltimore-Washington Expressway.

Meanwhile, more chartered buses were arriving. As the delegation from Alabama pulled into Washington, some of the passengers noted the banners on the sides of buses arriving from other parts of the country and wished they had banners, too. Then someone reminded them, "Can you see us getting through Alabama with signs all over these buses? We'll let 'em know who we are once we get to the Washington Monument."

Those in charge of placards were busy handing out the official march signs to the participants. WE DEMAND VOTING RIGHTS NOW! said some. Others read WE MARCH FOR FIRST CLASS CITIZENSHIP NOW!; WE MARCH FOR DECENT PAY NOW!; UAW SAYS END SEGREGATED RULES IN PUBLIC SCHOOLS; WE DEMAND AN END TO POLICE BRUTALITY NOW!; NO U.S. DOUGH TO HELP JIM CROW; and WE MARCH FOR EFFECTIVE CIVIL RIGHTS LAWS NOW! There was even a sign that said LOOK MOM! DOGS HAVE TV SHOWS. NEGROES DON'T! It referred to the fact that Lassie had a show on television, but there were no TV shows that had black characters. Every imaginable barrier to equal rights was protested in these signs. None but official signs or slogans were allowed, and none were in sight.

The area between the Washington Monument and the Ellipse behind the White House was the assembly area. It was a great chance for stargazing, since celebrities had turned out in great numbers: actors Marlon Brando, Sidney Poitier, James Garner, Burt Lancaster, Tony Franciosa, Paul Newman, Charlton Heston, Ruby Dee, Diahann Carroll, Frances Foster, and Joanne Woodward; singers Marian Anderson, Lena Horne, Odetta, Josh White, Lonnie Sattin, Joan Baez, Bob Dylan, Brook Benton, Bobby Darin, and Peter, Paul and Mary were there. The great baseball legend Jackie Robinson brought his son David to witness the historic occasion. Dr. Ralph J. Bunche, the first black American to win the Nobel Prize for Peace, for his work at the United Nations, was also there.

Josephine Baker, who wore her Free French Army uniform as a reminder that she had helped the French Resistance during World War II, made a short speech, saying she had returned to her native land because she wanted to be part of "this vast army of freedom." The comedian Dick Gregory told about a Chicago woman he knew who had worked at odd jobs to save up enough money to travel to Washington for the march. Burt Lancaster read a list of names of people in Paris who supported the march. Odetta, Josh White, and many others sang for the crowd. While the singers sang and the Hollywood celebrities gave short speeches, the crowd around the monument grew. The mood was festive; the air was filled with anticipation. But the sheer number of people began to strain the food, medical, and sanitary facilities to the breaking point.

Crowds lined up to sip from the drinking fountains and to use the portable toilets. People also flocked to the licensed food vendors' carts to buy hot dogs, sodas, and ice cream, which they preferred to the 80,000 cheese-sandwich bag lunches the church volunteers had made and were selling for fifty cents. Many felt the occasion was like a picnic that called for hot dogs and ice cream.

Fortunately, the good weather kept health problems to a minimum. Although sixty-six people suffering from the heat or exhaustion were sent by ambulance to hospitals, only four were ill enough to be admitted for treatment. There was not a single death at the march. Local health officials said that two or three deaths from heart attack or stroke would not have been unusual, given the size of the crowd and the age of some of the marchers. The biggest problem was getting sick people out of the crowd and to ambulances. In one case, an unconscious woman was passed person by person over the heads of the crowd to a cleared space where stretcher bearers were waiting.

Most people stayed healthy. They had come to march, and they found it hard to keep their feet still, especially once they saw more and more people arriving. Those who already had been there for hours began to wonder if they would get good spots at the Lincoln Memorial, where the main program was to take place. Some of them started to march early.

This was a development that Bayard Rustin, who had thought of just about everything else, had not considered. While the informal program at the Washington Monument was going on, and the crowd was gathering, the Top Ten were meeting with President Kennedy at the White House. The plan was that they would leave their meeting and travel to a point halfway between the Washington Monument and the Lincoln Memorial. The thousands of marchers would fall in behind them as they made their way to the Lincoln Memorial. The order of seating there had been carefully arranged beforehand.

Years later, Rustin explained,

> Now, one of the security measures that we had was that, here's the Lincoln Memorial, and in front of the Lincoln Memorial we were going to put the congressmen. Behind the congressmen we were going to put the honored guests—both reserved sections. Then, in order to create a sufficient distance between [them and] the ordinary, average person who was coming, we were going to have about twenty yards of the front all the way around filled in by trade unionists, so nobody could throw anything or start a fight—these were our people. So we had decided that at a quarter to one, these trade unionists would leave their positions and go and take the front areas, standing areas, all around before the honored guests and the congressmen came in. Well, people aren't so dumb. The minute they saw anybody moving, it dawned on them that these people were going to get the best seats! So they said . . . "We're going too!" So they start out. That was the one mistake we made.

Small groups of people stepped out onto Constitution and Independence avenues, followed by more groups. Just then, arriving from the White House to lead the march, the Top Ten realized the march had started without them! Whitney Young joked, "We'd better hurry up and catch up with our followers!" The Top Ten were hustled toward the head of the march. A. Philip Randolph was supposed to have walked alone, at the head of the march. But the seventy-four-year-old "elder statesman" who had proposed the march never made it to the front. He marched somewhere in the middle, a few steps behind the Confederate flag-draped coffin that symbolized the death of the old ways of segregation in the South.

The other leaders were close to the front. They walked hand in hand as the tide of people flowed along Constitution Avenue from the Washington Monument to the Lincoln Memorial.

Their wives did not march with them. Instead, the wives led a separate procession along Independence Avenue. If any of these women, or any other woman, objected, they did so in private. It is ironic how the secondary place of women was accepted without question on this day of protest against racial discrimination.

The third and last arrest of the day took place on Constitution Avenue, when a twenty-year-old Chicago man broke into the line of marchers and tore a placard.

As the last of the marchers left the area around the Washington Monument, Rustin's volunteers closed down the headquarters there. By the time the march began, there were about 200,000 people, and by the time the crowd had reassembled at the Lincoln Memorial it had swelled to at least 250,000. Helicopter police reported with amazement that there were some 1,500 buses in the specially reserved bus parking sections.

Just before the main program opened, Adam Clayton Powell, Jr., the black Congressman from Harlem and the powerful head of the House Education and Labor Committee, led the delegation from the House of Representatives to special seating at the other end of

March leaders walk hand in hand down Constitution Avenue. From left to right beginning with the third man from the left are Whitney Young, Roy Wilkins, A. Philip Randolph, and Walter Reuther.

the Mall, near the Capitol. Senator Hubert H. Humphrey led the Senate delegation. All together, the congressional delegation was huge, for as the idea of the march had caught on, and the estimated attendance rose, more and more members of Congress had decided they could attend after all. Those who attended felt it was a disgrace not to go, and they insisted that the names of the ninety-two members who stayed away be read into the Congressional Record.

There had never been a sight like it—a quarter of a million people, black and white, Jew and Gentile, grandparents and infants, male and female, rich and poor, powerful and powerless, walking shoulder to shoulder and hand in hand for a cause in which they believed. Many men and women wore black suits and dresses, as if to underscore the sense of dignity of the march. There were many clerical collars, too. For some, the blue-jean overalls worn by veterans of sit-ins were a special badge of honor.

The behavior of the crowd varied as well. Some laughed and sang, others carried looks of deep determination on their faces. Still others showed anger that they had to march a quarter million strong to have America take seriously their demands for equal rights.

Fifty-nine-year-old James Baker and thirty-year-old Jesse Gadson had come from Steubenville, Ohio, where they were steelworkers.

Among four hundred unskilled workers at their plant, only sixteen were black. Restaurants in Steubenville were segregated. The public schools had both black and white students, but no black teachers. They marched to protest those conditions.

Mike Sussman, a twenty-year-old white student, had no complaints about his own life. "I'm not looking out for myself; I'm looking out for the Negro," he explained. "This is something that everybody has to support, and not sit around and wait and see."

Albert Paxton, a black taxi driver, had decided to join the march on the spur of the moment. "It was a duty for me. I drove a cab for a while [Tuesday] evening, and then said, 'That's it. I'm going to Washington because it's a duty that has to be done.'"

Emily Rock, a black high school student, felt joy at being with so many people all committed to the same cause. "All around, in the faces of everyone, there was this sense of hope for the future—the belief that this march was the *big* step in the right direction. It could be heard in the voices of the people singing and seen in the way they walked. It poured out into smiles."

A white woman from South Carolina stood on the sidelines and watched the marchers pass. "I'm not sympathetic to all the purposes of this demonstration," she told a reporter for the *New York Post*, "but I must say they can teach this nation a lesson in good manners."

# CHAPTER 8

# I HAVE A DREAM

One of the great black leaders who had fought all his life for equal rights did not live to see the march. W.E.B. Du Bois had died in Ghana the previous day. Roy Wilkins, speaking for the NAACP, the organization Du Bois had helped to found, made the announcement over the huge loudspeakers.

Through his books and articles, and through his work on the NAACP publication *Crisis*, Du Bois had influenced many black Americans, including A. Philip Randolph and all the other civil rights leaders. He taught them to be proud of their blackness and to feel a kinship with their African homeland. He called his philosophy pan-Africanism. In his later years, tired of struggling for dignity in the United States, he made Africa his home.

Had he lived to see the march, Du Bois would have been impressed by its strong sense of dignity, as well as by the new sense of power that came from its sheer numbers and sense of right. Much had changed in America and the world since he had started working for black equality.

One of the most important changes was in communications. Television now made it possible for people to witness events in their own living rooms that were going on a continent—or even half a world—away. Many historians feel that television was one of the major tools of the nonviolent civil rights movement. Television viewers could see for themselves how racist whites attacked peaceful demonstrators. The conscience of America was struck by the injustice.

There was more TV coverage of the March on Washington than of any presidential inauguration. The forty TV cameras set up at the Lincoln Memorial represented the largest outdoor television operation that had ever been attempted. The major television networks were covering much of the march live and, through the new technology of satellite relay, carried it to Europe as well.

There were even "sympathy" demonstrations in other parts of the world—in London, Paris, Tel Aviv, and in Accra, Ghana, where W.E.B. Du Bois had lived. The All-China Federation of Trade Unions, with nine other Chinese organizations, sent a message of support for the march. Although in Cairo, Egypt, a demonstration at the U.S. Embassy by the African League was not permitted, Algerian premier Ahmed Ben Bella expressed his country's solidarity with the marchers and praised the Kennedy administration's efforts on behalf of racial equality.

There was no counting the number of still photographers. Not only did thousands of marchers bring cameras, but the national and

**The view from inside the Lincoln Memorial**

international press turned out in droves. *The Voice of America* carried radio broadcasts, live from the march, all over the world.

When the marchers reached the Lincoln Memorial for the main program of the day, all the major television networks switched to continuous live coverage. Never before had the glare of the public eye been trained on so many black people in such a public place.

Some who were not on the list of speakers were upset not to be included, among them the Reverend Fred Shuttlesworth, who had organized the civil rights campaign in Birmingham. Dr. King was concerned that his friend's feelings were hurt. But a greater cause for concern developed at the Lincoln Memorial.

After the march leaders reached the Lincoln Memorial, they mounted its steps and prepared for the main part of the program: the speeches. The crowd, meanwhile, assembled around the memorial. Some, having been on their feet all morning and then for the mile march, paused for a while to soak their feet in the Reflecting Pool between the Washington Monument and Lincoln Memorial. They had no way of knowing that trouble was brewing among the speakers.

At the eleventh hour new problems arose over the speech John Lewis of SNCC was to give. Walter Reuther, leader of the United Auto Workers, still felt it was too critical of the Kennedy civil rights bill. Archbishop O'Boyle still objected to the violent tone of some of the language, and threatened to walk off the podium if the speech was delivered as written.

To cover the loud shouting backstage, Bayard Rustin ordered that the National Anthem be played over the loudspeakers. Then he appointed an emergency truce committee to work out the problems—fast. Randolph, King, Lewis, and the Reverend Eugene Carson Blake of the National Council of Churches met in a guard station beneath the seat of Lincoln's statue, while Rustin persuaded Archbishop O'Boyle to go ahead with the invocation. Rustin promised the archbishop that he would be shown Lewis's speech in time to walk off the platform if he didn't like it.

# MARCH ON WASHINGTON FOR JOBS AND FREEDOM

## AUGUST 28, 1963

# LINCOLN MEMORIAL PROGRAM

**1.** The National Anthem — *Led by* Marian Anderson.

**2.** Invocation — The Very Rev. Patrick O'Boyle, *Archbishop of Washington.*

**3.** Opening Remarks — A. Philip Randolph, *Director March on Washington for Jobs and Freedom.*

**4.** Remarks — Dr. Eugene Carson Blake, *Stated Clerk, United Presbyterian Church of the U.S.A.; Vice Chairman, Commission on Race Relations of the National Council of Churches of Christ in America.*

**5.** Tribute to Negro Women Fighters for Freedom — Mrs. Medgar Evers
  Daisy Bates
  Diane Nash Bevel
  Mrs. Medgar Evers
  Mrs. Herbert Lee
  Rosa Parks
  Gloria Richardson

**6.** Remarks — John Lewis, *National Chairman, Student Nonviolent Coordinating Committee.*

**7.** Remarks — Walter Reuther, *President, United Automobile, Aerospace and Agricultural Implement Wokers of America, AFL-CIO; Chairman, Industrial Union Department, AFL-CIO.*

**8.** Remarks — James Farmer, *National Director, Congress of Racial Equality.*

**9.** Selection — Eva Jessye *Choir*

**10.** Prayer — Rabbi Uri Miller, *President Synagogue Council of America.*

**11.** Remarks — Whitney M. Young, Jr., *Executive Director, National Urban League.*

**12.** Remarks — Mathew Ahmann, *Executive Director, National Catholic Conference for Interracial Justice.*

**13.** Remarks — Roy Wilkins, *Executive Secretary, National Association for the Advancement of Colored People.*

**14.** Selection — Miss Mahalia Jackson

**15.** Remarks — Rabbi Joachim Prinz, *President American Jewish Congress.*

**16.** Remarks — The Rev. Dr. Martin Luther King, Jr., *President, Southern Christian Leadership Conference.*

**17.** The Pledge — A Philip Randolph

**18.** Benediction — Dr. Benjamin E. Mays, *President, Morehouse College.*

## "WE SHALL OVERCOME"

*Statement by the heads of the ten organizations calling for discipline in connection with the Washington March of August 28, 1963:*

"The Washington March of August 28th is more than just a demonstration.

"It was conceived as an outpouring of the deep feeling of millions of white and colored American citizens that the time has come for the government of the United States of America, and particularly for the Congress of that government, to grant and guarantee complete equality in citizenship to the Negro minority of our population.

"As such, the Washington March is a living petition—in the flesh—of the scores of thousands of citizens of both races who will be present from all parts of our country.

"It will be orderly, but not subservient. It will be proud, but not arrogant. It will be non-violent, but not timid. It will be unified in purposes and behavior, not splintered into groups and individual competitors. It will be outspoken, but not raucous.

"It will have the dignity befitting a demonstration in behalf of the human rights of twenty millions of people, with the eye and the judgment of the world focused upon Washington, D.C., on August 28, 1963.

"In a neighborhood dispute there may be stunts, rough words and even hot insults; but when a whole people speaks to its government, the dialogue and the action must be on a level reflecting the worth of that people and the responsibility of that government.

"We, the undersigned, who see the Washington March as wrapping up the dreams, hopes, ambitions, tears, and prayers of millions who have lived for this day, call upon the members, followers and wellwishers of our several organizations to make the March a disciplined and purposeful demonstration.

"We call upon them all, black and white, to resist provocations to disorder and to violence.

"We ask them to remember that evil persons are determined to smear this March and to discredit the cause of equality by deliberate efforts to stir disorder.

"We call for self-discipline, so that no one in our own ranks, however enthusiastic, shall be the spark for disorder.

"We call for resistance to the efforts of those who, while not enemies of the March as such, might seek to use it to advance causes not dedicated primarily to civil rights or to the welfare of our country.

"We ask each and every one in attendance in Washington or in spiritual attendance back home to place the Cause above all else.

"Do not permit a few irresponsible people to hang a new problem around our necks as we return home. Let's do what we came to do— place the national human rights problem squarely on the doorstep of the national Congress and of the Federal Government.

"Let's win at Washington."

SIGNED:

Mathew Ahmann, *Executive Director of the National Catholic Conference for Interracial Justice.*

Reverend Eugene Carson Blake, *Vice-Chairman of the Commission on Race Relations of the National Council of Churches of Christ in America*

James Farmer, *National Director of the Congress of Racial Equality.*

Reverend Martin Luther King, Jr., *President of the Southern Christian Leadership Conference.*

John Lewis, *Chairman of the Student Nonviolent Coordinating Committee.*

Rabbi Joachim Prinz, *President of the American Jewish Congress.*

A. Philip Randolph, *President of the Negro American Labor Council.*

Walter Reuther, *President of the United Automobile, Aerospace and Agricultural Implement Workers of America, AFL-CIO, and Chairman,* *Industrial Union Department, AFL-CIO.*

Roy Wilkins, *Executive Secretary of the National Association for the Advancement of Colored People.*

Whitney M. Young, Jr., *Executive Director of the National Urban League.*

*In addition, the March has been endorsed by major religious, fraternal, labor and civil rights organizations. A full list, too long to include here, will be published.*

## WHAT WE DEMAND*

1. Comprehensive and effective *civil rights legislation* from the present Congress—without compromise or filibuster—to guarantee all Americans

> access to all public accommodations
> decent housing
> adequate and integrated education
> the right to vote

2. Withholding of Federal funds from all programs in which discrimination exists.

3. *Desegregation of all school districts in 1963.*

4. Enforcement of the *Fourteenth Amendment*—reducing Congressional representation of states where citizens are disfranchised.

5. A new *Executive Order* banning discrimination in all housing supported by federal funds.

6. Authority for the Attorney General to institute *injunctive suits* when any constitutional right is violated.

7. A massive federal program to train and place all unemployed workers—Negro and white—on meaningful and dignified jobs at decent wages.

8. A national *minimum wage* act that will give all Americans a decent standard of living. (Government surveys show that anything less than $2.00 an hour fails to do this.)

9. A broadened *Fair Labor Standards Act* to include all areas of employment which are presently excluded.

10. A federal *Fair Employment Practices Act* barring discrimination by federal, state, and municipal governments, and by employers, contractors, employment agencies, and trade unions.

---

*Support of the March does not necessarily indicate endorsement of every demand listed. Some organizations have not had an opportunity to take an official position on all of the demands advocated here.

To stall for time, several dignitaries were asked to make brief remarks. Among them was Dr. Ralph J. Bunche, who in 1950 was the first black American to win the Nobel Prize for Peace, the recipient of which is decided on by a Norwegian parliamentary committee and is awarded each year by the Swedish king. He was a hero to black Americans, but he told the crowd, "The hero is you."

Rustin then sent Shuttlesworth out to make a few remarks, thus soothing Shuttlesworth's hurt feelings and buying a little more time. Meanwhile, in the huddle under Lincoln's seat, Blake objected to Lewis's use of words like "revolution" and "the masses," implying that they smacked of communist rhetoric. Randolph defended the terms, saying he himself had used them consistently for forty years. Blake backed down on that point and turned his objections to the "Sherman's march" passage. Randolph did not defend those words. King then spoke up. Referring to the "scorched earth" language in the text, he said, "John, I know you as well as anybody. That doesn't *sound* like you." He persuaded Lewis to let him change a few words. James Forman made the changes on a portable typewriter, also taking out some of the phrases he himself had put in.

Meanwhile, A. Philip Randolph addressed the crowd and was greeted by cheers. He was the "grand old man" of the struggle for black rights and was highly respected. His appearance at the microphones to give the first major speech of the afternoon also signaled the start of the main program. By now the crowd had been waiting long enough.

"We are gathered here in the largest demonstration in the history of this nation," Randolph began.

Let the nation and the world know the meaning of our numbers. We are not a pressure group, we are not an organization or a group of organizations. We are not a mob. We are the advance guard of a massive moral revolution for jobs and freedom.

This revolution reverberates throughout the land touching every city, every town, every village where black men are segregated, oppressed, and exploited.

But this civil rights revolution is not confined to the Negroes; nor is it confined to civil rights. Our white allies know that they cannot be free while we are not. . . .

Randolph then spoke of what the marchers wanted: the Fair Employment Practices Act, integrated public schools, a free democratic society. He stressed the intertwined goals of civil rights and economic equality. His voice rose, his hands waved in the air, and his face glowed when he ended by saying:

We here, today, are only the first wave. When we leave, it will be to carry the civil rights movement home with us, into every nook and cranny of the land. And we shall return again, and again, to Washington in ever-growing numbers until total freedom is ours.

A roar came up from the crowd as Randolph ended his speech. Many in the audience knew of his history with the March on Washington and shared his joy in seeing his dream come to be at last.

After the Reverend Eugene Carson Blake spoke, Randolph returned to the podium, to introduce the women of the civil rights movement who were to be honored. Four of the six women were activists: Rosa Parks had sparked the Montgomery bus boycott by refusing to give up her bus seat to a white man. Diane Nash Bevel, a teacher at Alabama State University in Montgomery, had written and distributed the first flier asking black Montgomeryites to boycott the buses because of Rosa Parks's arrest. Daisy Bates had helped prepare the black students who had integrated Central High School in Little Rock, Arkansas, in 1957, and also had helped to organize SNCC. Gloria Richardson of Cambridge, Maryland, had formed the Cambridge Nonviolent Action Committee earlier in the year to force integration of restaurants, bowling alleys, and other public accommodations.

The two remaining women had lost their husbands to the cause of civil rights: Myrlie Evers's husband, Medgar Evers, had been assassinated that spring. Mrs. Herbert Lee also had been widowed by the civil rights movement. Herbert Lee, a fifty-two-year-old farmer in McComb, Mississippi, and an active member of the NAACP, had been shot in September 1961 by a white segregationist who resented Lee's work in getting blacks to register to vote.

When John Lewis finally stepped up to the microphones to deliver his speech, it had been greatly rewritten. Archbishop O'Boyle quickly looked it over and did not walk off the platform. Lewis was nervous. But he soon warmed up, and the crowd warmed to him. It was common knowledge that he had been arrested and beaten dozens of times. Of all the leaders, though the youngest, he had suffered the most at the hands of Southern police. When he spoke of being "in constant fear of a police state," the crowd knew he was speaking from experience.

"My friends," he said,

let us not forget that we are involved in a serious social revolution. By and large, American politics is dominated by
politicians who build their careers on immoral compromises
and ally themselves with open forms of political, economic,
and social exploitation.

There are exceptions, of course. We salute those. But what
political leader can stand up and say "My party is the party of
principles?" . . . Where is *our* party? Where is the political
party that will make it unnecessary to march on Washington?
Where is the political party that will make it unnecessary to
march in the streets of Birmingham?

Lewis closed by calling out a long list of cities where demonstrations had taken place, his voice taking on the cadences of a preacher.
This was a rephrasing and a toning down of the lines that Archbishop
O'Boyle had found most offensive. The new lines read: "We will
march through the South, through the streets of Jackson, through the
streets of Danville, through the streets of Cambridge, through the
streets of Birmingham. . . . But we will march with the spirit of love
and with the spirit of dignity that we have shown here today." When
he finished, the crowd stamped and cheered.

Walter Reuther, president of the United Auto Workers, was next
on the program. He said, in part:

To me the civil rights question is a moral question that
transcends partisan politics, and this rally today should be the
first step in a total effort to mobilize the moral conscience of

America and to ask the people in Congress of both parties to rise above their partisan differences and enact civil rights legislation now.

Now the President—President Kennedy—has offered a comprehensive and moderate bill. That bill is the first meaningful step. It needs to be strengthened. It needs F.E.P.C. [Fair Employment Practices Commission] and other stronger provisions. And the job question is crucial; because we will not solve education or housing or public accommodations as long as millions of American Negroes are treated as second-class economic citizens and denied jobs.

Reuther was to have been followed by James Farmer, national director of CORE, but Farmer was in a Louisiana jail. So Floyd B. McKissick, CORE's national chairman, read a message from Farmer:

> From a south Louisiana parish jail, I salute the march on Washington for Jobs and Freedom. Two hundred and thirty-two freedom fighters jailed with me in Plaquemine, Louisiana, also send their greetings.
>
> I wanted to be with you with all my heart on this great day. My imprisoned brothers and sisters wanted to be there too. I cannot come out of jail while they are still in; for their crime was the same as mine—demanding *freedom now*. . . .
>
> Some of us may die, like William L. Moore [a white postman from Baltimore, Maryland, who had been shot to death in northeastern Alabama on April 23, 1963, while carrying a sign urging Equal Rights for All during a walk from Tennessee to Mississippi] or Medgar Evers, but our war is for life, not for death, and we will not stop our demand for 'FREEDOM

NOW.' We will not . . . stop till the dogs stop biting us in the South, and the rats stop biting us in the North.

After a musical selection provided by the Eva Jessye Choir and a prayer given by Rabbi Uri Miller, president of the Synagogue Council of America, Whitney Young, Mathew Ahmann of the National Catholic Conference for Interracial Justice, and Roy Wilkins gave their speeches. These remarks were formal and followed the approved texts exactly.

Then Mahalia Jackson stepped to the microphone to sing an old

Mahalia Jackson

spiritual born of the slave experience, "I Been 'Buked and I Been Scorned." It told of the rebukes and scornful treatment black people had suffered for so long:

*I'm gonna tell my Lord*
*When I get home,*
*I'm gonna tell my Lord*
*When I get home,*
*Just how long you've*
*Been treating me wrong.*

The song, and Jackson's powerful rendition, brought many to tears. It was a hard act to follow. When Rabbi Joachim Prinz, president of the American Jewish Congress, replaced Jackson on the podium, he said, "I wish I could sing." He then recalled the Holocaust, in which millions of European Jews and others were killed by the Nazis while millions of non-Jews stood silently by:

When I was the rabbi of the Jewish community in Berlin under the Hitler regime, I learned many things. The most important thing that I learned in my life, and under those tragic circumstances, is that bigotry and hatred are not the most urgent problem. The most urgent, the most disgraceful, the most shameful, and the most tragic problem is silence.

A great people, which had created a great civilization, had become a nation of silent onlookers. They remained silent in the face of hate, in the face of brutality, and in the face of mass murder.

America must not become a nation of onlookers. America

must not remain silent—not merely black America, but all of America. It must speak up and act, from the President down to the humblest of us, and not for the sake of the Negro, not for the sake of the black community, but for the sake of the image, the dream, the idea, and the aspiration of America itself.

When Dr. Martin Luther King, Jr., stepped up to speak, the shadows were lengthening on the Mall and the marchers were tired. But as King was introduced, the crowd stirred with expectation.

King faced an endless sea of faces and a huge press corps. He spoke formally and stuck to the text of his speech. Although at informal meetings, and in church, he was known to take off on the wings of words and soar to great heights, he was not a preacher on this occasion. He was acting the part of a major civil rights leader on an important day.

But then he got to this part of his speech: "We will not be satisfied until justice rolls down like waters and righteousness like a mighty stream," and allowed his voice to rise and fall as he did when he preached, and when he did so, the crowd responded with such emotion that he knew he could not read the next lines.

He had planned to say, "And so today, let us go back to our communities as members of the international association for the advancement of creative dissatisfaction." But he knew that it was time to build on the emotion of the crowd. And so he started to preach, making it up as he went along.

I say to you today, my friends, that even though we face the difficulties of today and tomorrow, I still have a dream. It

Martin Luther King, Jr., delivers his famous "I have a dream" speech.

is a dream deeply rooted in the American dream. I have a dream that one day this nation will rise up and live out the true meaning of its creed—we hold these truths to be self-evident, that *all* men are created equal.

I have a dream that one day on the red hills of Georgia, the sons of former slaves and the sons of former slaveowners will be able to sit down together at the table of brotherhood. . . .

I have a dream my four little children will one day live in a nation where they will not be judged by the color of their skin but by the content of their character. I have a dream today!

I have a dream that one day, down in Alabama . . . little black boys and black girls will be able to join hands with little white boys and white girls as sisters and brothers. I have a dream today!

Then he talked about faith and asked everyone to let freedom ring from the mountainsides, saying:

Let freedom ring from the prodigious hilltops of New Hampshire . . . from the mighty mountains of New York . . . from Stone Mountain of Georgia . . . from every hill and molehill of Mississippi, from every mountainside, let freedom ring.

And when this happens, when we allow freedom to ring, when we let it ring from every village and every hamlet, from every state and every city, we will be able to speed up that day when *all* of God's children—black men and white men, Jews and Gentiles, Protestants and Catholics—will be able to join hands and sing in the words of the old Negro spiritual, "Free at last, free at last, thank God Almighty, we are free at last."

Standing from left to right: Mathew Ahmann, Joachim Prinz, John Lewis, Eugene Carson Blake, Floyd B. McKissick, Walter Reuther. Seated from left to right: Whitney Young, Cleveland Robinson, A. Philip Randolph, Martin Luther King, Jr., Roy Wilkins.

As King moved quickly to allow A. Philip Randolph to give his closing remarks and Dr. Benjamin Mays, president of Morehouse College, to give the benediction, the huge crowd was silent for a moment, so overcome were they by King's speech. Then in a huge rush of emotion they cheered and wept openly. Randolph and Mays had to wait several minutes for calm to return before they could close the program.

In living rooms across the country, some eighty million Americans had the same reaction as the crowd at the Lincoln Memorial. Few people had ever heard King give a complete speech. The majority were struck with awe at the power of his words.

For many, there was a sense of regret: "I wish I was there"; "I should have gone myself." But all were glad to share the experience, even from afar.

Two of the proudest listeners were A. Philip Randolph and Dr. Benjamin Mays. Standing together on the podium looking out over the crowd, the two elderly men silently gave thanks that they had lived to see such a moment.

The younger march leaders were overjoyed as well. As five o'clock came and the crowd began to leave, right on schedule, one of the leaders reportedly turned to Bayard Rustin and said, "Rustin, I have to hand it to you. You're a genius."

March leaders meet with President Kennedy after the march. From the right: Roy Wilkins, Walter Reuther, Lyndon Johnson, John F. Kennedy, A. Philip Randolph, Joachim Prinz, John Lewis, Martin Luther King, Jr., Whitney Young, Mathew Ahmann.

# CHAPTER 9

# AFTERMATH

By previous arrangement, the Top Ten went immediately after the march to the Cabinet Room at the White House, where President Kennedy greeted them. When Martin Luther King, Jr., walked in, the president smiled and said, "I have a dream." This was both a compliment to King on his speech and a way of acknowledging that Kennedy understood the importance of his dream. Uncomfortable with Kennedy's praise, King asked if he had heard the excellent speech of Walter Reuther. Kennedy answered, "Oh, I've heard him plenty of times." Like most Americans, Kennedy had never before heard a complete King speech, and he was both moved and impressed.

But the march leaders were not there to give or receive compliments. The march had been successful beyond their wildest dreams, and they wanted to use its power to push for a stronger civil rights bill. Randolph asked the president to agree to add a section banning discrimination in employment. He was worried about the effects of joblessness on black teenagers. He told the president, "I may suggest to you that they present an almost alarming problem because they have no faith in anybody white. They have no faith in the Negro leadership. They have no faith in God. They have no faith in government. In other words, they believe the hand of society is against them."

Walter Reuther wanted the attorney general to be able to bring lawsuits against those who denied anyone their civil rights. Robert Kennedy would not make any promises.

When the meeting broke up, all the march leaders were tired and looking forward to a rest, but they, and the president, had reporters to meet. Kennedy praised the march and the marchers:

> We have witnessed today in Washington tens of thousands of Americans—both Negro and white—exercising their right to assemble peaceably and direct the widest attention possible to a great national issue. . . .
>
> One cannot help but be impressed with the deep fervor and the quiet dignity that characterize the thousands who have gathered in the nation's capital from across the country to demonstrate their faith and confidence in our democratic form of government. . . .
>
> The executive branch of the federal government will continue its efforts to obtain increased employment and to eliminate discrimination in employment practices, two of the prime goals of the march. . . .
>
> This nation can afford to achieve the goals of a full employment policy—it cannot afford to permit the potential skills and educational capacities of its citizens to be unrealized.

The cause of twenty million Negroes has been advanced by the program conducted so appropriately before the nation's shrine to the Great Emancipator, but even more significant is the contribution to all mankind.

As Kennedy spoke, the marchers who had participated in the historic day were heading back to their everyday lives. The Lincoln Memorial program had ended on schedule, so there was still plenty of daylight left. The marchers trooped back to their waiting buses and parked cars and special trains to begin the long journey home. Although they were tired, in the words of an old Southern black saying, their souls were rested. They would always remember this day, and in years to come would tell their children and grandchildren and great-grandchildren, "There was a great March on Washington, and I was there."

For the march organizers and their volunteers, there was much yet to be done. While the crowds were still leaving, sweepers began cleaning up debris from the fast-emptying Mall. Tons of trash were removed in a matter of a few hours. Portable toilets were packed up; portable drinking fountains were readied to be loaded on trucks. Loudspeaker wires were unstrung from trees; microphones and chairs were removed from the makeshift podium in front of the Lincoln Memorial. Hats and sunglasses and other personal belongings were collected and placed in a March on Washington lost and found.

Meanwhile, reporters rushed to meet story deadlines and photographers went to their darkrooms to develop the hundreds of pictures they had shot. All the stories stressed the huge size and amazing peacefulness of the march, and since in those days blacks were all but invisible on the staffs of the major media, almost all the stories were written by whites:

"Their triumph was one of discipline, of good manners and good sense," wrote the reporter for *The Daily Sketch*.

> This tense city had feared violence . . . but there was none. Police had nothing more to do than stare at the banners—"No U.S. dough to help Jim Crow grow"—and listen to the song—"We Shall Overcome."

Claude Sitton, of *The New York Times*, reported:

> Few who saw the marchers or talked with their leaders could be but impressed by their enthusiasm, determination and confidence. Few could but ask if the seeming resignation with which many Negroes once accepted their place in American society had disappeared forever. . . . Now [the Negro's] leaders' statements, his own militant behavior and the new light in which others see him show that he is no longer an interested bystander in the civil rights struggle. Today's appeal to Congress and the nation, more than anything else, served notice that the Negro believes that he is as much a master of his destiny as any American.

In the *New York Post*, Stan Optotowsky noted:

> Probably the greatest public relations triumph was provided by the marchers themselves. Their dignity, good humor and pleasant sincerity created an image which the American

white can grasp. The white may not identify with the bitter rock-throwers in Birmingham or battered students in Montgomery. But he can understand the plight of a portly 40-year-old Negro with a wife and three children who wants to stay in the best motel he can afford.

United Auto Workers president Walter Reuther said after the March that this "was the beginning of a broad policing of conscience." That was the aim—to get Americans to do more than tut-tut on the plight of Little Rock [Arkansas] school children and to start thinking about the basic rights to which Negroes are entitled as citizens.

And Kay Boyle, who covered the march for *Liberation*, wrote:

It aroused one to gentleness, to forbearance, and at the same time to commitment from which there can be no turning back. I lost two of my children, and my friends, in that enormously gentle and goodnatured crowd, and I could not get close enough to see the speakers, but their voices, and their presence, filled the church-like hush under the trees. And I knew that if one was American, and believed in the equality of man, on the 28th of August, 1963, there was no other place to be.

Many newspapers carried excerpts from King's speech or from those of other march leaders. Most, including the Atlanta *Daily World*, carried photographs of King on their front pages the next day. The Atlanta paper's policy had been never to put a picture of King on the front page. More than any other event, King's speech at the March on Washington catapulted him to national prominence.

White supremacist groups felt they had to respond to the march. James Venable, chairman of the National Knights of the Ku Klux Klan, announced plans for a mass rally at Stone Mountain, near Atlanta, Georgia, shortly afterward. It would be "the White man's answer" to the march, said Venable, who expected 6,500 Klansmen from forty-six states to attend. In actuality, only a few hundred people showed up.

Other white racists decided to respond to the peaceful march, and to the changes that were taking place in the South, with violence. On September 9, the first day of school in Birmingham, Alabama, three public schools opened under court order to admit black students for the first time. Governor George Wallace sent Alabama National Guardsmen to bar the black students. President Kennedy then federalized the Guard, taking over command, and withdrew the troops from Birmingham. The city was filled with tension.

The next Sunday, September 16, was the annual Youth Day at the Sixteenth Street Baptist Church in Birmingham. Four girls, all fourteen years old, left Bible class early and were in the basement ladies' room. They were talking excitedly when a loud explosion shook the church. All four girls were killed.

On November 22, President Kennedy visited Dallas, Texas, with his wife, Jacqueline Bouvier Kennedy, to campaign on behalf of the candidacy of John Connally for governor of Texas. While riding in a motorcade, Kennedy was shot and killed by Lee Harvey Oswald. Malcolm X, stating that the hatred in America over race had killed the president, said it was a case of "chickens coming home to roost." The remark was seen as untimely and unsympathetic. The Honorable Elijah Muhammad, leader of the Nation of Islam, officially silenced

Malcolm X. It was the beginning of a rift between them that eventually ended with Malcolm X's leaving the National of Islam. He formed his own group and stopped calling whites devils; in fact, he invited whites who wanted to help the black cause to work with him.

After Kennedy was assassinated, Vice President Lyndon B. Johnson was sworn in as president. He vowed to push through the Kennedy civil rights program. In January 1964 the nation ratified the Twenty-third Amendment to the Constitution, which outlawed the poll tax, a set amount of tax to be paid as a prerequisite for voting. Many southern states and localities had used the poll tax as a way to keep blacks from registering to vote, because when they tried to register, they had to pay the tax—all of it at once—for every year since they had turned twenty-one.

On July 2, 1964, President Johnson signed into law the most far-reaching civil rights legislation passed since the Reconstruction period. The Civil Rights Act of 1964 contained measures that the Top Ten had pushed for at and after the March on Washington, including the cutting off of federal funds from programs that discriminated against blacks.

The act also contained provisions to help guarantee blacks the right to vote, but they still were not strong enough to force Southern states to comply. In 1965 Dr. Martin Luther King, Jr., and the SCLC began a voting rights campaign in Selma, Alabama, that was greeted with more white violence. In response President Johnson introduced, and Congress passed, the Voting Rights Act of 1965.

A. Philip Randolph had predicted that federal civil rights laws would soon be passed. These two pieces of legislation—the 1964

Civil Rights Act and the 1965 Voting Rights Act—would in a few short years turn around the whole political and social system of the South.

That same year, on February 21, 1965, Malcolm X was assassinated in New York City, and four Black Muslims were arrested, tried, and convicted of his murder. By the time of his assassination, Malcolm X had become even more famous and, after his break with the Black Muslims, more accepted in both the black and white communities than he had been at the time of the March on Washington.

By that time, a major split had occurred in the civil rights movement. Many members of SNCC never forgave the other leaders for watering down John Lewis's speech. SNCC as a whole became alienated from the rest of the civil rights movement. A new, more militant leadership took over, and in 1966 the new executive director of SNCC, Stokely Carmichael, issued a call for "Black Power!"

SNCC was not especially clear as to what Black Power meant. Its leaders were talking about economic and political power. But the slogan sounded violent and brought to the minds of many images of armed struggle. It replaced "I have a dream" as the slogan of the movement in the minds of the American people.

Once the 1964 Civil Rights Act and the 1965 Voting Rights Act had been passed, the legal bases for the end of segregation were in place. The civil rights battle in the South shifted to the courts. A long struggle was ahead, but eventually many blacks in the South would be able to vote and elect blacks to office.

Just as Randolph had predicted, the stage of race relations then shifted to the North, to which the civil rights movement previously had not paid much attention. When blacks in many Northern cities rioted in the summer of 1964, Martin Luther King, Jr., and others realized that blacks in the Northern cities had been little touched by the legal victories that had been won. They, too, lived in segregated housing and went to segregated schools, but Northern segregation was harder to fight. It was not segregation under the law but segregation by housing patterns and custom.

King tried to take the tactics of nonviolent protest to Northern cities like Chicago, but with little success. Northern urban blacks were more likely to be influenced by Stokely Carmichael's talk of Black Power than by King's talk of nonviolent struggle. King also lost support when he began to speak out against American involvement in the Vietnam conflict. He criticized President Johnson's policies in Vietnam because of his belief in nonviolence and also because a disproportionate number of American soldiers fighting in Vietnam were poor and black.

More and more, King was enlarging his focus to include poor people of all races. In 1968 the SCLC decided to hold a Poor People's March on Washington to dramatize the plight of the poor. King was in the middle of planning for the march when striking black sanitation workers in Memphis, Tennessee, asked him to lead a march in support of their cause. King agreed to do so, and while in Memphis, on April 4, 1968, he was assassinated by James Earl Ray.

Two months later, on June 5, 1968, Senator Robert F. Kennedy, the former U.S. attorney general, was in Los Angeles, California, campaigning for the Democratic presidential nomination. He was assassinated by Sirhan Sirhan.

Although conspiracies were suspected in all the assassinations of the 1960s, none were ever proved. In each case, the final conclusion was that the assassin or assassins had acted alone. But there seemed to be a climate of hate in the United States in the 1960s. Of the major players in the March on Washington, three—the two Kennedys and King—were killed within five years of the march; none was more than forty-six years old.

A. Philip Randolph, father of the March on Washington, died a natural death in 1979 at the age of ninety. His trusted deputy, Bayard Rustin, died in 1987 at the age of sixty-five. Randolph's dream of greater civil rights marches on Washington, D.C., which he had voiced in his speech at the march, did not come true.

Even if there had never been a March on Washington for Jobs and Freedom, the Civil Rights Act introduced by President Kennedy would have been passed. The tide had turned; the conscience of white America had been pricked. But the march remains a high point in the history of the struggle for black civil rights. It was a dignified demand for equal rights that will never be forgotten and remains an inspiration to people of all races.

Following the passage of the Civil Rights and Voting Rights acts, black voters registered in great numbers throughout the South. Today blacks are an important voting bloc there. Black voters have elected black mayors, black police chiefs, and black school board members. John Lewis, formerly of SNCC, was elected to the Atlanta City Council in 1981 and then to the U.S. House of Representatives in 1986. In 1990 L. Douglas Wilder was elected governor of Virginia, becoming the first black governor to serve in any state since the Reconstruction period.

Many other blacks hold positions of power and authority in business, the arts, and higher education. In 1963 the black middle class was a tiny group; since then it has grown steadily. But there is still a large population of poor, uneducated blacks in the hollows of the South and in the big-city ghettos of the North. They have equality under the law but not in fact. And even the most educated and prosperous blacks face discrimination. They are still judged by the color of their skin, not by the content of their character.

America still has much to do to see that the dream behind the March on Washington is fulfilled.

# BIBLIOGRAPHY

**Books**

Adams, John A., and Joan Martin Burke. *Civil Rights: A Current Guide to the People, Organizations, and Events.* New York: R. R. Bowker Company, 1970.

Branch, Taylor. *Parting the Waters: America in the King Years 1954–1963.* New York: Simon & Schuster, 1988.

Farmer, James. *Lay Bare the Heart: An Autobiography of the Civil Rights Movement.* New York: Arbor House, 1985.

Garrow, David J. *Bearing the Cross: Martin Luther King, Jr., and the Southern Christian Leadership Conference.* New York: William Morrow & Co., 1986.

Haskins, Jim. *The Life and Death of Martin Luther King, Jr.* New York: Lothrop, Lee & Shepard, 1978.

McKissack, Patricia, and Frederick McKissack. *A Long Hard Journey: The Story of the Pullman Porter.* New York: Walker & Company, 1989.

Parks, Rosa, with Jim Haskins. *Rosa Parks: My Story.* New York: The Dial Press, 1991.

Ploski, Harry A., and James Williams, eds. *The Negro Almanac: A Reference Work on the Afro American.* Fourth edition. New York: John Wiley & Sons, Inc., 1983.

Rustin, Bayard. *Down the Line: The Collected Writings of Bayard Rustin.* Chicago: Quadrangle Books, 1971.

Saunders, Dorie, ed. *The Day They Marched.* Chicago: Johnson Publishing Co., 1963.

Wilkins, Roy, with Tom Mathews. *Standing Fast: The Autobiography of Roy Wilkins.* New York: The Viking Press, 1982.

Williams, Juan. *Eyes on the Prize: America's Civil Rights Years, 1954–1965.* New York: The Viking Press, 1987.

## Articles

"Biggest Protest March," *Ebony*, September 1963, pp. 29ff.

Boyle, Kay, "No Other Place to Be," *Liberation*, September 1963, p. 9.

"Excerpts From Addresses at Lincoln Memorial During Capital Civil Rights March," *The New York Times*, August 29, 1963, p. C21.

"Inside the March on Washington," *Jet*, September 12, 1963, pp. 14–33, 50–61.

"Leader of March a Man of Dignity," *The New York Times*, August 29, 1963, p. C20.

McGrory, Mary, "A Gentle Spirit Prevails at March Born in Protest," *New York Post*, August 29, 1963, p. 36.

"Marchers Sing and Voice Hope on Way to Capital," *The New York Times*, August 29, 1963, p. C19.

"On the March," *Newsweek*, September 2, 1963, pp. 17–21.

Optotowsky, Stan, "The Marchers' Aim Was to Rouse a Nation," *New York Post*, August 29, 1963, p. 5.

Phillips, Cabell, "Food Facilities Overburdened; Marchers' Illnesses Are Minor," *The New York Times*, August 29, 1963, p. C19.

"President Thanks Demonstrators," *The Christian Science Monitor*, August 30, 1963, p. 3.

Ryder, Vincent, and David Shears, "200,000 in Civil Rights March," *London Daily Telegraph and Morning Post*, August 29, 1963, pp.1ff.

"Seeds of Liberation . . . The First Wave," *Liberation*, September 1963, pp. 6–8.

Sitton, Claude, "3½-Year-Old Protest Movement Comes of Age in Capital March," *The New York Times*, August 29, 1963, p. C20.

"They March in Their Massed Thousands to His Shrine," *Daily Sketch*, August 29, 1963.

Toth, Robert C., "Only 3 Arrested, Including a Nazi," *The New York Times*, August 29, 1963, p. C20.

## Other Sources

The Bayard Rustin Archives, Bayard Rustin Fund, Inc., New York, NY.

Columbia University Oral History Program, Columbia University.

# IMPORTANT DATES IN CIVIL RIGHTS HISTORY

## 1909

National Association for the Advancement of Colored People (NAACP) founded by W.E.B. Du Bois and other influential blacks and whites; organization is incorporated in 1910

## 1910

National Urban League founded by influential blacks and whites to help Southern blacks newly arrived in Northern cities

## 1917

Ten thousand blacks march down Fifth Avenue in New York City to protest racial discrimination

## 1925

Brotherhood of Sleeping Car Porters (BSCP) organized by A. Philip Randolph

## 1936

*December 8:* NAACP attorneys file first suit in campaign for equal pay for black teachers

## 1941

*June 18:* A. Philip Randolph and others meet with President Roosevelt about their proposed March on Washington on July 1 to protest discrimination in war industries

*June 25:* President Roosevelt signs Executive Order 8802 forbidding discrimination in war industries; Randolph calls off the march

*December 7:* Japanese bomb U.S. naval base at Pearl Harbor, Hawaii; United States enters World War II

## 1942

Congress of Racial Equality (CORE) founded by James Farmer and others in Chicago

## 1945

*August 14:* World War II ends

## 1946

*June 3:* U.S. Supreme Court bans segregation on interstate buses

*December 5:* President Truman creates Committee on Civil Rights

## 1947

*April 9:* CORE sends first Freedom Rider group to test the Supreme Court ban on segregation in interstate travel

## 1948

*July 26:* President Truman issues Executive Order 9981 mandating equality of opportunity in the armed forces, effectively integrating troop units

## 1951

NAACP begins attack on "separate but equal" education

## 1954

*May 17:* U.S. Supreme Court in *Brown v. Topeka Board of Education* rules that racial segregation in public schools is unconstitutional

## 1955

*December 1:* Rosa Parks is arrested in Montgomery, Alabama, for refusing to give up her bus seat to a white man; the Montgomery Bus Boycott begins December 5

## 1956

*November 13:* U.S. Supreme Court upholds a lower-court decision banning segregation on Montgomery, Alabama, city buses; Dr. Martin Luther King, Jr., and other boycott leaders call off the boycott a month later after gaining concessions from the bus company

## 1957

*February 14:* Southern Christian Leadership Conference (SCLC) organized, with Dr. King as president

*May 17:* Prayer Pilgrimage to Washington, D.C.; King gives his first speech to a national audience

*August 29:* Congress passes the first civil rights act since Reconstruction

*September 24:* President Eisenhower orders federal troops to Little Rock, Arkansas, to prevent interference with school integration

## 1960

*February 1:* Students in Greensboro from North Carolina Agricultural and Technical State University sit in at Woolworth lunch counter; by February 10 the movement has spread to five other southern cities

*April 15–17:* Student Nonviolent Coordinating Committee (SNCC) organized

*May 6:* President Eisenhower signs Civil Rights Act of 1960

*October:* Dr. King arrested for sitting in at lunch counters in Atlanta, Georgia, and given a harsh sentence; Democratic presidential candidate John F. Kennedy calls Coretta Scott King to express his sympathy

*November:* John F. Kennedy elected president

## 1961

*May 4:* CORE launches a series of Freedom Rides into the South

## 1963

*April 3:* Dr. King opens antisegregation campaign in Birmingham, Alabama

*August 28:* More than 250,000 persons participate in the March on Washington for Jobs and Freedom

*September 15:* Sixteenth Street Baptist Church in Birmingham, Alabama, bombed, killing four young black girls

*November 22:* President Kennedy assassinated in Dallas, Texas; Lyndon B. Johnson becomes president

## 1964

*July 2:*  Civil Rights Act signed by President Johnson

## 1965

*February 21:*  Malcolm X assassinated in New York City

*March 21–25:*  Dr. King leads march from Selma to Montgomery, Alabama, to demand voting rights

*August 4:*  President Johnson signs Voting Rights Act

## 1966

*June:*  Stokely Carmichael, head of SNCC, issues a call for "Black Power!"

*August 5:*  Dr. King attacked as he leads a march through Chicago's South Side

*August 11–16:*  Blacks riot in Watts section of Los Angeles

## 1967

*March 25:*  King attacks U.S. policy in Vietnam at Chicago march

*June 13:*  Thurgood Marshall, former NAACP lawyer, nominated as first black Associate Justice of the U.S. Supreme Court; confirmed by Senate August 30

*July 20–23:*  Black Power conference in Newark, New Jersey, attracts largest and most diverse group of black American leaders ever assembled

*November 7:*  Carl Stokes of Cleveland, Ohio, and Richard Hatcher of Gary, Indiana, are the first blacks to be elected mayors of major American cities

## 1968

*March 4:*  Dr. King announces he will lead a Poor People's March on Washington in April

*March 28:* Dr. King leads a protest march in support of striking sanitation workers in Memphis, Tennessee

*April 4:* Dr. King assassinated by James Earl Ray in Memphis

*April 11:* President Johnson signs the Civil Rights Bill banning discrimination in housing and making it a crime to interfere with civil rights workers

*May 2:* Ralph David Abernathy, King's successor as head of the SCLC, leads Poor People's March on Washington, D.C.

*June 5:* Senator Robert Kennedy is assassinated in Los Angeles while campaigning for the Democratic presidential nomination

## 1977

*January 31:* Andrew J. Young, first black American ambassador to the United Nations, presents his credentials to U.N. Secretary General Kurt Waldheim

## 1984

Jesse Jackson seeks the Democratic presidential nomination

## 1986

*January 15:* Martin Luther King, Jr., birthday celebrated as a federal holiday for the first time

*November 4:* John Lewis is elected to the U.S. House of Representatives

## 1990

*November 7:* L. Douglas Wilder of Virginia becomes the first black governor of any state since Reconstruction; David N. Dinkins becomes the first black mayor of New York City

# Illustration Credits

Grateful acknowledgment is made to the following organizations and individuals for permission to reproduce the illustrations which appear in this book:

The John F. Kennedy Library, for pp. 27 and 110.

The New York Public Library, for pp. 9, 36, and 39.

The Bayard Rustin Fund, Inc., for pp. 52, 56, and 95–97.

The Schomburg Center for Research in Black Culture, The New York Public Library, Astor, Lenox and Tilden Foundations, for pp. xvi, 3, 6, 17, 22, 41, 47, 72, 87, 88, 90, 93, 106, and 108.

Flip Schulke, photojournalist, for pp. 79 © 1976, 81 © 1976, 103 © 1992, and 121 © 1992.

Don Uhrbrock, *Life* magazine, for p. 44 © Time Warner, Inc.

# INDEX

Page numbers of photographs appear in *italics.*